This Page Left Blank?

Andi Swift is a man eminently equipped to write about chasing and realizing dreams: he has lived some of his already and has stayed positive and faith-filled in the face of setbacks as he has pursued others. Where dreams have become reality for Andi, it is not just the luck of the draw, it is because Andi has shaped the skills and attitudes that make for success in the natural and produce fruit in the spiritual.

Whether it's in your work, the church or your family, life lived out of vision is always better than life lived by process and routine, but it also requires us to take deliberate steps, one at a time. Perhaps reading this book and learning from Andi's experiences is one of your steps.

Christen Forster, River Church, Maidenhead

The future belongs to those who see it before it happens. It is one thing to have a dream; it is a totally different thing to see that dream become a reality. The reason why so many Christians are frustrated with their station in life is that there is no understanding as to how to bring that God-given dream to fruition. In this book, Andi skilfully sets out the pathway to the fulfilment of those dreams. Keep dreaming because your future is waiting for you to write it.

Mark Pease, El-Shaddai International
Christian Centre, Bradford

Andi Swift is an outstanding individual with a heart to see people achieve their highest goal. He is a young man awakened to kingdom possibility. I highly recommend that you read this book! It will inspire and provoke you to not only find your dream, but also outwork it.

Dreams are incredibly important; they are the fuel that ignites the heart of anyone who wants to live beyond themselves, to achieve and burn bright. They are the things that cause us to break through all kinds of challenges and difficulties. Without a dream I believe we are but mere shadows. But without a plan our dream remains just that, a dream. We need a plan to get it working, to get it moving.

In this book these are the things that Andi explains to us so well: the finding and birthing of a dream and then becoming the kind of person that is able to fulfil the outworking of that dream, both spiritually and naturally. This is a great read for everyone! Awesome job, Andi!

Mark Stevens, Abundant Life Church, Bradford

Andi is a man who loves to dream God-dreams. This book is a practical challenge to help you find God's dream for your life.

Andy Frost, Share Jesus International

In the absence of focus, any path will do. In this excellent book, Andi Swift invites the readers to plot their course and chart their progress based on God-given aspirational dreams and goals. Required reading for those who take their destiny seriously.

John Glass, General Superintendent,
Elim Pentecostal Churches

The future belongs to the dreamer who has the passion to make it happen. In this book, Andrew shows us the importance of having a dream and holding on to that dream until it comes into reality. As Christians, we should always have big dreams because we serve a big God. Living the dream in whatever God has called us to is one of the most important things in our lives. This book gives some powerful insights and practical equipping in living this kind of life – well done, Andrew, keep dreaming!

Gavin White, King's Church, Greater Manchester

Andi has tapped into an idea that is rooted in Scripture and yet often overlooked. The idea is that we of all people can dream big dreams because we serve a great God, who is working in us, both according to his will and for his good pleasure. Thanks for the reminder, Andi.

Brian Brodersen, Calvary Chapel Costa Mesa, CA, USA

Dreaming is something people have forgotten how to do. This book can inspire people to dream afresh and grasp the truth that we all have a 'blank page' waiting to be written upon with whatever we plan, dream and believe for in life. Go for your dream and never give up!

Christian Allsworth, New Generation Church, Belfast

One of Andi's passions in life is surfing. His second love is riding a wave, which is really what this book is about. His enthusiasm and passion for God makes him a man who truly wants to ride the wave and inspire others to do the same. Read the book and catch the wave.

Al Bullen, Fusion

In a world of such mediocrity it is refreshing to be called to live beyond oneself and pursue one's dreams. There are many self-help, 'live your dream' books out there, but Andi anchors his in the Word of God and the will of God. Andi has been personally tested and shaped by broken dreams, but his testimony shows that setbacks and struggles are not the end of the story.

Brett Davis, Christian Surfers International
International Director, Coledale Australia

This Page Left Blank?

Fulfilling your purpose in life

Andrew Swift

Authentic

First published 2011 by Authentic Media Limited
Presley Way, Crownhill, Milton Keynes, MK8 0ES
www.authenticmedia.co.uk
Company Registration No: 7101487

British Library Cataloguing in Publication Data

A catalogue record for this book is available from the British Library

978-1-85078-895-9

Cover Design by DesignLeft (www.designleft.co.uk)
Printed in Great Britain by Cox and Wyman, Reading

CONTENTS

This book is dedicated to anyone who has shaken off the dust and decided to pursue their dreams. You can make it!

You see things, and say 'Why?' But I dream things that never were, and I say 'Why not?'
George Bernard Shaw

Acknowledgements

I would like first to acknowledge my wife, Vicki, and our children, Anna, Bethan and Reuben, who are a great source of encouragement as well as my refuge. Thank you for believing in the beauty of my dreams.

During the writing of this book my family and I went through one of the biggest storms of our lives, and I want to acknowledge everyone that walked with us. Thank you specifically to pastors M. and H. Pease who so diligently fed us the Word of God, and to C. and J. Forster for their faithfulness in the use of their prophetic gifting. Finally, to everyone who supported us in encouragement and gifts – you know who you are. We are eternally grateful and feel so blessed to have friends and family like you.

To my proofreaders, Jan Vickers and Mary Bunker, thank you for your attention to detail as well as your overwhelming patience.

Special thanks to my personal editor, Sam Casey – I thank you and deeply appreciate all that you did in making this book a success. You allowed the Holy Spirit to use your creative talent and attention to detail.

Thanks also to everyone at Authentic Media Limited, especially my copy-editor, Jess Bee.

The biggest thanks goes to God: my friend, Father, and my Jehovah-Jireh, who has provided for all my needs. I love and adore you!

Foreword

For as he thinks in his heart, so is he.

Prov. 23:7, NKJV

Now to Him Who, by . . . the power that is at work within us, is able to . . . do superabundantly, far over and above all that we [dare] ask or think [infinitely beyond our highest prayers, desires, thoughts, hopes, or dreams] – To Him be glory in the church and in Christ Jesus throughout all generations forever and ever. Amen.

Eph. 3:20,21, AMP

You and I were designed to dream. As we see from these two portions of Scripture, dreams are the very seedbed of our future, the imaginations of everything we can have, become and achieve mapped out on the canvas of our mind. Dreams are the vehicle through which we visit our future before it ever happens. Everyone has the ability to dream and thus change their future. As Dr R. Mumba, a colleague of mine, says, 'the future belongs to those who can see it before it happens'.

You might be dreaming right now about the person you want to become, the one you will marry, the exploits you will do, the children you will have.

Historical and biblical figures have turned this world upside down because of the dream birthed inside them to see things differently. Martin Luther King's famous speech inspired millions of people across a nation to seek and embrace change.

Dreams that at the time seemed so far-fetched and unrealistic have resulted in some of the most spectacular technological and scientific advances humankind has ever seen, by people such as Einstein, Alexander Graham Bell and the Ford brothers.

Some of the world's most significant businesses and social enterprises started from the small seed that was a dream and now have become realities that impact millions of lives.

The dreams that some of our elite sportsmen and women had as children, harnessed with application and diligence, have seen them develop into expert practitioners in their chosen field. But again it all started with a dream of being on that podium and receiving that trophy.

In life your dream will be challenged, but nothing of significance will ever happen without your commitment to dream. To dream is the first step to greatness, and the book you are holding right now is a tool that will inspire you not only to excel in the arena of your dreams, but to establish them and see them come to fruition.

This book was written by a man I have known for twenty-five years; a man with entrepreneurial energy who has achieved great things as a businessman, a family man and a Christian. A man of great personal integrity who I have grown to respect for his commitment to the God he sees and the God who inspires. Andrew has the ability to dream big and to pursue things until they become a reality. Take heart, be wise, dream again and let the practical principles of this book walk you to the place of fulfilled dreams.

For too long society has belittled those who dream, whereas in actual fact, dreaming is one of the most powerful things that we can do as human beings.

Dream big and live large.

Let the journey commence!

Mark Pease, Senior Pastor
El-Shaddai International Christian Centre, Bradford

1

Dreams

A man is not old until regrets take the place of dreams.
John Barrymore

One thing that is really inspiring for me is the sight of a person of advanced years running a marathon or taking part in a triathlon. It is mind-boggling to hear stories of people running marathons at the age of ninety-eight, ninety-nine and even a 100 years old. Each of these athletes has a similar attitude: 'Age is simply a state of mind; my next target is . . .' They remain positive and focused on their dreams. It's wonderful because they still have dreams, ambitions and targets in life. Despite their age, they haven't grown old because they are still dreaming.

I believe at every stage in life, whether you are eight or eighty, you should have dreams – and pursue them. In life there is always someone demanding your attention, or circumstances that can distract you from living your dream. If you can keep hold of yours, your future is ripe with potential.

My elder daughter has somehow managed to collect a whole host of really old VHS tapes. Her vast collection includes a copy of Disney's *Cinderella*, the classic story of a downtrodden young woman forced to play servant to her bitter stepmother and demanding stepsisters. The video is so worn out it jumps. The sound keeps fading and the picture is terrible, but nevertheless my daughter sings along to every song and knows every line. One of her favourites is 'A Dream Is a Wish Your Heart Makes' which talks about how dreams are places where wishes come true and heartache disappears.

Despite her predicament, Cinderella clings to her dream of a better life. As the story unfolds, her dreams come true and, like all good fairytales, she ends up living happily ever after, having, of course, married the handsome prince.

Whether a four-year-old realizes it or not, the Cinderella story delivers a brilliant message about dreams. As adults, it should encourage us to pursue ours wholeheartedly. Cinderella asks the same question that many of us may ask ourselves: 'Why not me? Why shouldn't I marry the prince?' Your dream may not be to live in a castle with a handsome prince, but do you ever get the feeling, like Cinderella, that there is more to life than what you know? That you are meant to do something extraordinary? That you are destined to be someone who makes a difference? Like Cinderella, we should allow ourselves to nurture big dreams; dreams that fill us with hope, that inspire us and that make us wonder. Without dreams, we simply end up going through the motions. Life becomes about existing rather than living. If you don't pursue your dream, the chances are that you will find yourself, by accident, somewhere you don't want to be.

We should allow ourselves to daydream. How and what we dream is based on our experiences of life; the things we read, especially the Word of God, and what people say or don't say to us. Dreams are the product of sensory experiences, as well as what's on our heart and mind. A dream is something that inspires us personally or corporately; something that drives us from the inside, a vision we get when we look at tomorrow and consider what we could accomplish.

Each of our dreams is personal: you may dream of seeing a church established in Timbuktu, having a family, gaining a qualification, building a school in Kenya, giving lavishly to your church building project, or simply enjoying life by sailing around the South Pacific or diving in the Red Sea.

You only have to look at the number of talent shows now dominating prime-time television to realize the emphasis that society places on dreams. I remember watching a pizza delivery man, who had never performed in front of an audience before, taking to the stage to sing on one such show. He was phenomenal. After his performance he said that he had always dreamed of singing on stage and how he now felt complete. It was really moving, not just because he had just delivered an amazing rendition of 'Bring Him Home' from *Les Miserables*, but because after fantasizing for so long about singing on stage, he was now living the dream. Whatever your dream, it can be a powerful catalyst in your life.

History is proof of the value of dreams. It is full of accounts of people who created seismic shifts because they allowed themselves to dream big. One of history's best known and best articulated dreams belonged to Dr Martin Luther King Jr. His heart's desire – for a world in which all races coexisted harmoniously as equals – formed the basis of one of the most powerful public speeches ever recorded. The 'I Have A Dream' speech was a defining moment in the American Civil Rights Movement. And its power derived from the fact that it painted in profound words the dream he held in his heart.

Dr King was actually delivering a prepared speech when someone in the crowd shouted, 'Tell them about the dream, Martin!' From that point, he did not require the script because what he went on to say was etched on his heart. It was merely the vocal expression of a dream that had been fermenting in him for many years.

Dr King would have been amazed at what has happened in less than fifty years since he was shot dead on 4 April 1968, which was that in 2001, an African-American, Colin Powell, would become Secretary of State, and then in 2009, another African-American, Barack Obama, would enter the White House as America's forty-fourth president. President Obama's inauguration, at the Lincoln Memorial in Washington DC, may never have been possible had it not been for the words Dr King spoke to a crowd of thousands near the very same spot more than forty-five years earlier. We can now stop speaking about the dream he espoused, as the dream speaks for itself.

We cannot know the precise origins of Dr King's dream, but clues may be found in his education and the beliefs he held. He was extremely well-educated; he was so bright that he graduated at the age of nineteen with a BA in Sociology. He then went on to study at the Crozer Theological Seminary where he gained a BA in Theology. After his studies, he became the pastor of Dexter Avenue Baptist Church and in 1955 he gained his PhD in Systematic Theology from Boston University, USA.

He lived at a time when there was explicit and inhumane segregation between blacks and whites; even as a six-year-old, he was separated from his playmates because of the colour of his skin. Shortly after Dr King received his doctorate, a bus boycott was organized and he was appointed its leader.

The nature, the values and the character of God that Dr King read about, studied and heard every Sunday from childhood were all reflected in the dreams he started to foster. He saw with his own eyes the injustice and inequalities that had created deep divisions in American society, and he knew that this wasn't God's heart for humankind. Just like Dr King, I believe that as we read and absorb the Word of God, our minds and emotions are changed and that this affects the actions we take, the choices we make and the course of life we follow. Ultimately, it determines whether or not we achieve our dreams.

Dreams are a great motivator. Cinderella imagined herself dancing in the castle to motivate her and to keep her from becoming disheartened. She made a determined effort not to let her dire circumstances chip away at her dreams.

One difference between ourselves and Cinderella is that we don't have a fairy godmother to help us fulfil our dreams. Rather, we have someone much more powerful – a real, constant, omnipotent Father God. And God's heart for each one of us is that we live life to the full:

> The thief comes only in order to steal and kill and destroy. I came that they may have and enjoy life, and have it in abundance.
> John 10:10, AMP

This abundance isn't just about finances or wealth. God's abundance for each of us covers our job, our ministry, our 'fun' time, our family, our relationships and our health. Like petrol in an engine, dreams can be the fuel that drives us forward. God's heart for us in this is abundance – until it overflows. We are told in the Bible that we are made in the image of God. One of God's key characteristics is creativity; he created the world in six days, having conceived it in his imagination. The very nature of God is to create something from nothing:

> In the beginning God created the heavens and the earth. Now the earth was formless and empty, darkness was over the surface of the deep, and the Spirit of God was hovering over the waters.
>
> Gen. 1:1,2

As we are made in God's image, it is also our prerogative to conceive in the mind, to dream. It's a God-given ability and a gift that we need to utilize and act upon.

In my last book, *My Reason For Hope*, people from all walks of life shared the hope that they have found in Christ Jesus. They shared how this hope has changed their lives and, in most cases, their perspective of life. We have a fantastic hope of eternal life, but God still wants us to enjoy our time here on earth. He not only wants us to enjoy life, but he wants us to live it to the full and in abundance. Thanks to God-given free will, what we do with our lives is really down to the choices we make and the personal decisions about which dreams to pursue and, indeed, whether we pursue any dream at all. Like the unmarked canvas standing in front of the oil painter, we are born with a blank page on which to work. It is up to us to make choices about how we fill that page based on the gifting God has given us, the knowledge we acquire and a fuller understanding of God's will.

Dreams can profoundly affect our actions and the way we respond to life's challenges. They can affect some of the simplest decisions in life. As we walk along life's road we constantly make choices about which way to turn. We hear preaching on finding out the will of God for our lives. We may read books about our purpose. Are our dreams at odds with God's will for us, or do they help us to identify God's purpose for our life?

I believe God's Word. I believe God wants us to live our dreams:

> Trust in the LORD and do good; dwell in the land and enjoy safe pasture. Delight yourself in the LORD and he will give you the desires of your heart. Commit your way to the LORD; trust in him and he will do this.
>
> Ps. 37:3–5

There is a saying: 'The poorest man isn't a man without a cent, but a man without a dream.' Even the penniless man has something if he has a dream. Later in the book I'll share some of my dreams and how, in the face of losing everything, my dreams survived.

Do you have a dream? What is your dream? Are you pursuing it, or have you laid it to rest because circumstances have taken over, or because it's so far out of sight? I want to encourage you not to throw in the towel. Whatever your past or present circumstances, you are capable of determining your own future. As Eleanor Roosevelt said, 'The future belongs to those who believe in the beauty of their dreams.'

Through this book I want to challenge you, first, to discover your dreams, and then, to pursue your dreams wholeheartedly, to overcome the obstacles and challenges you face and not to give up. Don't be left asking 'What if ...?' Success only comes by turning dreams into reality, so we need to keep dreaming big. I will encourage you to consider some of the dreams you have. Are you still pursuing them? Have well-intentioned peers told you that your dreams are silly or out of reach? God's heart for you is to fulfil your desires, your dreams, and for you to live in abundance, to the full. God is the God of the impossible. If that is the case, then it means we should live as if there are no limitations. You can reach your goals; you can fulfil your earthly destiny and your dreams. Just trust in the Lord and delight yourself in him:

> But seek first his kingdom and his righteousness, and all these things will be given to you as well.
>
> Matt. 6:33

2

This Page Left Blank?

The pages are still blank, but there is a miraculous feeling of the words being there, written in invisible ink and clamouring to become visible.
Vladimir Nabokov

'This page left blank' – it's a paradoxical phrase. If you are old enough, you will recall it written on exam papers or in technical manuals. Its use was a necessary quirk of the printing processes used at the time.

The phrase really struck a chord with me when I started to consider my own destiny, and whether it was God's will that I press forward in achieving my own personal dreams and ambitions. Was my future predestined, or were these dreams a clue to God's purpose for my life? I asked myself if my life really was an empty canvas, a blank page. Or was there a picture painted on the page of my life by God, a picture he wanted me to discover? As I really started to think about it, I recalled attending a youth conference as a teenager during which the preacher very skilfully and visually showed the audience how God's plans for our lives are often far bigger than we ever achieve or even imagine. He pulled a piece of paper from his pocket, folded as small as he could make it. He suggested that, when you get to heaven, this folded piece of paper would be shown to you by God. He would say, 'Well done, good and faithful servant, this is what you have achieved.' But then, the preacher said, he would open up the paper to its full size and say, 'But this is what I had in store for you, if only you had pursued your dreams.' But what are the dreams God has for us?

I want to make it clear that I'm not saying we should simply pursue every thought that comes into our heads. There is a difference between a hare-brained idea and a God-given dream. Later on in this book, I will share how to identify whether a dream is from God or not – it's all down to understanding how God has wired us, whilst using our discernment. My hope is that you receive encouragement to consider that you have everything you need to fulfil God's plans for your life, and those plans are often in the very make-up of who you are.

A newborn baby's life may appear to stretch out before it like a blank page, ready to be filled with its own experiences, choices and designs. But I believe there is more to life than that. To use an analogy, my young daughters have painting books that simply require water to be brushed onto the paper. When they do so, the previously invisible colour emerges and a hidden picture is revealed. Like these hidden paintings, I believe God has already created a design for our lives, even before we were formed in the womb. But this wonderful picture only starts to appear as we pour the water of his Word and his Spirit into our lives.

God has instilled in us certain gifts and abilities and placed us in a certain location, at a certain time, in order that we can fully become the beautiful picture that he intended us to be. We have been given everything we need to achieve what God has intended for us. Whether we fulfil his purpose, though, depends on the choices we make and a decision about whether or not we follow his will.

If you feel like a blank page devoid of anything beautiful, I want to tell you that God chose you long before you decided to follow him. You were chosen to be fruitful. He has plans for your life that will lift you up. You are called to be blessed and to be fruitful in all that you do. The painting hidden in your life is waiting to be revealed. It's a painting of beauty. But it requires you, first, to respond to God's call on your life, to repent of your sin and to acknowledge Jesus as your Lord and Saviour.

Until you do that, you will not have access to the paintbrush or the water pot necessary to uncover the beauty that God has in store. When we accept Jesus into our lives, we say, 'I place you as my Lord and Saviour, I am ready to get rid of sin, to remove the blemishes on my painting. I allow you, God, to pour the water of your Spirit on my life so that my painting may be revealed. I know the painting was always there; the road was already mapped out. Now I know it's my responsibility to walk the road you have for my life. I commit to discovering and revealing your painting.'

A common mistake is to reduce God to a human level, to suppose that he is limited by the same boundaries that we as human beings face. Churches have started to incorporate secular psychology and philosophy into their teaching. Human rationale has replaced instruction based on the Word of God. Yet God is profoundly beyond our understanding. He is the all-powerful one, to be worshipped and adored. He is the same yesterday, today and forever. He chose us and he has a plan and purpose for our lives.

When we ask Jesus to be our Lord and Saviour we give him space to work anew in our lives. We are no longer lost souls, but are reborn as new creations. When we choose to follow God, we are instantly able to access everything we need for life and godliness. However, it's all a process, and so we have to train our minds and our hearts to live this way. It's easy to tell you to go after your dream, but I know we all have dreams that have been shattered, or that we feel will never come to pass. We all face tough times in our lives, but this is where faith comes in. We have to believe what God has said in his Word. We must say to ourselves that the things we put our hands to will be blessed and be successful if they are in accordance with what God wants. Why? Because it is written in the Word:

> The LORD will perfect that which concerns me; Your mercy and loving-kindness, O LORD, endure forever – forsake not the works of Your own hands.
>
> Ps. 138:8, AMP

When we live life with the full and complete understanding of what God has done for us, something wonderful happens. The rules of the world no longer apply. Instead, God's abundant work begins. He will take the things that we consider worthless in our lives and create something that is precious. He takes the things that concern us and perfects them. He is the God of multiplication, not division. He turns ashes into beauty, things that are dead into life. He chooses to work with the weak things of the world. We read in Amos 9:13,14 that God has promised that the ploughman will overtake the reaper. For this to happen in one season there would have to be such an abundant harvest that the crops still require harvesting when the ploughman returns the following season. So if you are looking forward to a time of fruitfulness and harvest in your life, get ready to be fruitful before you even start to plough your field. God is not confined to working within the boundaries of human limitation. I'm not saying, 'become a Christian and everything will be all right'. The principals I'm addressing here are simply the heartbeat of God. If we believe what it says in Amos 9, and allow these words to grow our faith, influence our actions and how we pursue our dreams, things will change.

In his book *Outliers*, Malcolm Gladwell explains why he believes some people achieve so much more than others. It is, he says, more than about who they are and what they are like; instead it has more to do with the culture they grow up in and the way they spend their time. In the many examples he gives, he details the seemingly extraordinary coincidences that are common to those who enjoy success. For instance, he explains that almost all successful Canadian hockey players are born in the first few months of the year. Being born in these months allows them to grow up bigger and stronger than their counterparts as they are the oldest in their academic year. Gladwell goes on to explain the path to success of prominent business leaders and sports stars. In doing so he demonstrates that success is more to do with who an individual associates with and, more importantly, the time and culture they are born into, than their education.

Gladwell's book is an eye-opener in showing why certain people succeed. But the one thing I believe it fails to identify is the multiplication effect that a life following God can have. God can move past the natural into the supernatural. He is not restricted by culture, circumstances or human relationships. The dreams you have can come true, in spite of your natural circumstances. He can give you a harvest where you have not planted. But you need the seed of the Word of God in you so that you have the full resources available to you as you move into your dreams and uncover the painting that God has placed on your life.

As children, we are like the blank page. But as we grow older we begin to discover the innate skills and ambitions God has given us. We then start to uncover the invisible picture that was there on the page of our life before we were even conceived; we discover God's plan for our life. In order to uncover the picture, we need to allow the Word and the Spirit of God to direct our paths and per-form the multiplication effect in our lives as we choose to obey him. It's our choice whether to follow God, to allow the picture to be revealed:

> Choose for yourselves this day whom you will serve, whether the gods your forefathers served beyond the River, or the gods of the Amorites, in whose land you are living. But as for me and my household, we will serve the LORD.
>
> Josh. 24:15

3

Finding Your Dream

Only believe, only believe;
All things are possible, only believe.
Daniel Paul Rader

Do you have a dream?

I believe that we all have dreams, whether we are able to express them or not. Most human beings want to make a difference in the world. Right now you may not know what your dreams are, or you may not feel able to articulate them, but that doesn't mean they don't exist. Discovering your dream will be like adding fuel to a fire. You will start to burn with desire and hope.

How do we discover our dreams? It is easy to expect to receive clear spiritual direction, but God is not a compass. He is more interested in what he will do in our lives, how he will transform us. He has planted in us hopes, passions and gifts that will generate dreams that inspire us. Dreams are extremely important. Whether you have a big dream or consider your dreams to be small, it really doesn't matter. What matters is that you have a dream at all. Do you simply want to watch the world go by? Life is too short to miss out on the joy of fulfilling some of your dreams and, ultimately, God's purpose for your life, which is often intertwined with that.

Apathy is one of the biggest barriers to discovering your dreams – allowing yourself simply to go through the motions of life: waking up, going to work from Monday to Friday, having a little fun on Saturday and routinely showing up at church on Sunday; it is easy to accept the status quo. You may simply settle for your promise of a place in heaven and live a simple life that appears adequate to outsiders. On the inside you may deeply yearn to pursue your dreams. Maybe it is so long since you allowed yourself to dream that you can no longer remember what it was that you once fantasized about.

Secretly you may feel disappointed that, whilst you have faith in Jesus, your life seems meaningless. You may rationalize that your lost dreams were a victim of circumstance, of your worldly responsibilities, like raising a family or having a mortgage.

So how do you find your dream, or revive a dream you had when you were younger? Revitalizing your dreams is often as simple as talking through your aspirations and your deepest desires with someone dear to you; knowing that they will not laugh in your face if they seem far-fetched or beyond what they would consider achievable.

There is a US TV series called *Chuck*, about a computer nerd who works at an electronics store and who unwittingly has sensitive government secrets implanted in his brain. Chuck lives a double life, fighting terrorists one day, working at the Buy More store with his best friend Morgan the next. In one episode there is a great dialogue between Morgan and his girlfriend, Anna. Anna teases out of Morgan the dream he once held, but had laid to rest because he didn't think he was good enough to achieve it. The conversation takes place after Morgan is tricked into becoming deputy manager of the store. He has been trying to hold the staff together but finds his friends have turned against him when the manager wants to fire them:

Anna: Why do you care if this store holds together?

Morgan: What do you mean?

Anna: I mean, don't you have some goal in this world outside this store; even Jeff and Lester have their ridiculous band. Don't you have a dream, Morgan?

Morgan: Yes, of course I do, it's just . . .

Anna: What?

Morgan: It's crazy, and you will laugh at me.

Anna: No, no, no, I promise I will not laugh.

Morgan: Promise? . . . I want to be a Benihana chef, in Hawaii . . . I know, it's stupid.

Anna: No, no, no, Morgan, it's not stupid, it's totally attainable.

Morgan: No, it's not, Anna. You have to train for, like, years, OK? I'm way past my prime, I'm not Asian. And I don't even know where to get the knives.[1]

Morgan later quits his job and asks Anna to join him in going to Hawaii, where he wants to learn the ancient cooking art of Hibachi.

Morgan had lived with a secret dream for many years. Only when he told someone about it, however, did he start to turn it into a reality. We all need to articulate our hidden dreams. Those people who truly love us will support us, no matter how ridiculous our aspirations may seem.

Be careful, too, not to belittle the dreams of others. Children, especially, have the imagination to develop wonderful dreams that can be crushed just as easily by throwaway comments and hurtful words, however unintentionally. When I was four years old, a teacher told me that I would end up in jail. Imagine how those words can affect a young mind. Nearly thirty years later, I still remember vividly how it made me feel: undervalued, ignored and judged without a trial.

Encourage your loved ones to find and pursue their dreams. Speak words of affirmation and hope to them. Free your children to dream; allow them to experience life. Encourage them in reading and meditating on the Word because that will help them to develop their own dreams.

Here are some useful things you can do to discover your dreams:

Let Creation Inspire You

There is no more profound example of the results a dream can inspire than creation itself. If you struggle to allow yourself to dream, spend time in God's beautiful creation. Immersing yourself in the world around you can be a hugely liberating and inspiring experience. I love surfing and when I'm sitting on my board, whether it's in California or Devon, in the midst of creation, there is a tangible sense of God's presence. In the film *The Power of One*, the main character, P.K., goes into the African bush to consider his destiny and is inspired to start teaching English. Like a drop of water that becomes a waterfall, he sees that if he can teach one person he will eventually change a nation. Spending time in God's creation allowed him to be inspired. Creation stirred the passion that was already in him.

Let People Inspire You

God's creation is not just confined to the hills and mountains, the seas and rivers, the flora and fauna. It also extends to his most treasured possession: people. God's people are rich in variety. Spending time among some of the vast array of cultural, ethnic and social groups will open your eyes and awaken new dreams in life. It will allow you to develop an understanding of God's worldview. His heart is all about redemption, about seeing all people come to acknowledge Jesus as their Lord and Saviour. Experiencing the world will help you understand this worldview.

I have had the benefit of going on several life-changing trips to far-flung places. At a young age, my parents encouraged me to go on a mission trip to Hungary and Romania, shortly after the collapse of the Communist regime. Before I had left school, I had seen with my own eyes what it was like to live without running water and waste disposal. On another trip, I lived in the Indian jungle for a month, building a retreat for the locals, but it was the abject poverty of the cities I visited like Chennai, Coimbatore and Otty that I will remember forever.

Even my business trips to the Middle East have had a profound effect on me. In places like Egypt and Jordan, poverty is apparent everywhere you look. In the affluent Emirates, many people are seduced by the external extravagances of wealth, but if you look below the surface you find abject poverty, especially in the out-of-sight labour camps for migrant construction workers.

If you have the opportunity to do so, I would recommend travelling to different countries as a way to broaden your horizons and give yourself a new perspective on life. You will never be the same again. Organizations like

Scripture Union and World Horizons provide advice about lots of different mission trips, and there are many opportunities throughout the world to get involved. If you are unable to travel, there are plenty of ways to get your hands dirty right on your doorstep. Charities like Shelter, which helps homeless people, may be able to give you the chance to move in circles that you may never do otherwise.

God has given us our eyes and ears to see and hear what is going on around us. Travelling the world and beginning to understand the cry of people's hearts will inspire us to dream. The dream may not even be connected to what we have experienced. That doesn't matter. The imperative is that our hearts and minds are challenged and changed. Shortly after returning from India I started a skateboard competition for the people of the town I lived in. I also launched a cross-denominational youth event. Neither of these was directly connected in any way to my experience in India, but they happened as a result of a renewed passion and awakened dreams, and a conviction that I could make a difference. I had determined that I was not going to be apathetic, but a person of action.

Let Individuals Inspire You

Get around people who inspire you:

> As iron sharpens iron, so one man sharpens another.
>
> Prov. 27:17

If you haven't got a dream, spend quality time with Word-infused people who do have a dream; their passion will rub off on you. Spend time with people who have chosen not to wait until something happens, but who have decided to make it happen with all the ability and anointing that God has given them, based on their knowledge of the Word of God.

If you can spend time with a person who is truly anointed and seeks to live God's way, you will be challenged and inspired. You should be able to find these types of people in a good Bible-based church. What do these people see in you? Do they recognize a particular gifting? Their input could help you to unlock your dreams.

One of the main concerns for any church leader is how to tap into people's potential, how to empower them to achieve their aspirations and dreams. A church should be a place where everyone is told that they can do it, that they can make it.

If you were taught that you had unlimited resources, what would your dream be? What would you set your sights on? Let yourself think like this for a moment. If there were no limitations, no boundaries, where would you picture yourself? What would you be doing?

Recognize Who You Are

Understanding yourself is key. What is it that makes you, you? Not the job you do, not the things you do, but who you are on the inside. What are you like when you close the door, when no one else is about? What gets you excited? What are you passionate about? What makes you laugh and cry? What occupies your mind? What are the thoughts you can't shake? What makes you tick? God wired you in a certain way; you're different to everyone else; you are unique. God placed things in you that no one else has. If you listen to your heart, what does it say? Paying attention to these things will often uncover hidden dreams that have the fingerprint of God on them.

What are you gifted in? What abilities and interests do you have? These are often a clue to why God put you on the planet. Pinpointing your destiny doesn't have to be painful; simply looking at the things that come naturally can help you to unlock your dreams.

Keeping Up With The Joneses

There is always going to be someone with more money than you, someone with a bigger car or a nicer house, more exotic holidays and a more powerful job. Equally, there will always be people, who have fewer things and aren't so successful, who look up to you. Keeping up with the Joneses is not what we are about. Dreaming big is not just about how much material wealth you acquire or what status you can achieve.

In all your dreaming you need to seek first the kingdom of God. His desire is to see all people come to the knowledge of him; our dreams should reflect this.

Risk-Taking

I approach life with passion and large helpings of get-up-and-go. Consequently, I dream big and I'm not afraid to take risks. Fortunately, Vicki, my wife, supports me wholeheartedly. In contrast, she isn't a natural risk-taker; she's much more analytical, more logical. She thinks things through methodically, and this is reflected in the fact that her dreams are much less radical. She dreams of camping holidays and big family Christmases – different dreams to mine, but important nonetheless. That's the key: everyone's dreams are important and they all need encouragement and support, however radical.

A dream can be found simply by saying to yourself that you will not stay within your comfort zone and you will start to take a few risks:

To laugh is to risk appearing the fool.

To weep is to risk being called sentimental.

To reach out to another is to risk involvement.

To expose feelings is to risk exposing your true self.

To place your ideas, your dreams before the crowd, is to risk being called naïve.

To love is to risk not being loved in return.

To live is to risk dying.

To hope is to risk despair, and to try, to risk failure.

But risks must be taken because the greatest hazard in life is to risk nothing.

The person who risks nothing does nothing, has nothing, and becomes nothing.

He may avoid suffering and sorrow, but he simply cannot learn and feel and change and grow and love and live.

Chained by his certitudes, he is a slave, he's forfeited his freedom.

Only the person who risks all that he cannot keep, to gain that which he can never lose, is truly free.[2]

To find your dreams you need to get into a position to receive them. Like Habakkuk in the Old Testament, you need to place yourself at your watchtower and listen to God. Get around people who inspire you, get into a church that encourages you to pursue your dreams with the full and complete understanding of God's Word. His Word will help to inspire your dreams, but be prepared to take risks with the knowledge that God will perfect the things that concern you (Ps. 138:8). In other words, as we take a risk, we do so with the faith that God is with us, the risk is mitigated by the fact that we have God by our side. However, taking a risk, is a risk – we can still fail. But, at least we will have tried, and at least we will have stepped out of our comfort zone. Later on we will look at how to handle failure.

Like Martin Luther King Jr., our dreams are the product of our experiences in life, coupled with a knowledge of God's Word. Each of us is different. We have all experienced different things in life and we have all been exposed to different cultures, situations and circumstances. All of these affect the dreams we nurture. God placed you in a specific time and place so that, first, you may discover your dream and, second, acquire the tools to fulfil it.

4

Destiny Versus Destination

When we embrace what lies within, our potential knows
no limit. The future is filled with promise, the present rife
with expectation. But when we deny our instinct, and
struggle against our deepest urges, uncertainty begins.
Where does this path lead? When will the changes end? Is
this transformation a gift or a curse? And for those that
fear what lies ahead, the most important question of all:
can we ever change what we really are?
Opening voiceover, *Heroes*, Season 1, Episode 13

As I encourage you to pursue your dreams, you may ask
how they fit in with your God-given destiny. We read a lot
about the ideas of destiny and purpose and, if you are like
me, you have probably struggled with the notion at some
point in your life. There have been times when I have lain
awake at night asking myself if I'm living the will of God:
if I'm in the right career, the right city, the right house. We
waste a lot of time thinking and talking about destiny, the
will of God and our purpose in life. It can cause us unnec-
essary frustration and worry. Life is about much more
than this. You don't need to buy books or watch DVDs on
destiny and discovering the will of God for your life.
Destiny isn't about the size of your payslip or how much

influence you have in business or politics. It is living the life God called you to; that's the best place you can be. What God wants you to do is linked to what he wants to do in your life. As a child of the 1970s and 1980s, living in a great Christian home and attending a good charismatic church, the main emphasis was on our destiny being a place in heaven. I remember songs like Mark Altrogge's 'I Have a Destiny' and old southern gospel songs like 'Everyone Will Be Happy Over There' or 'Headin' for Gloryland'. There is nothing wrong with these fantastic songs – they are based on the Word – but the impression they leave is that our only destiny is heaven. There is an alternative view: heaven is our destination, but destiny is something different. There is much more to life than death. End-time theology teaches us much but, as the Bible says, tomorrow will take care of itself:

> Therefore do not worry about tomorrow, for tomorrow will worry about itself. Each day has enough trouble of its own.
>
> Matt. 6:34

We have a destiny in the here and now. We don't want to get to the end of our lives and be left wondering what we could have done if we'd given ourselves the chance.

Some people might think that there is an inherent contradiction in encouraging you to pursue your dreams whilst reminding you that you have a God-given destiny here on earth. But the two things are not mutually exclusive, in fact, they go hand in hand. Our innate desires, our innate abilities to achieve certain things, those things that are so ingrained that they are almost a part of our DNA, are all God-breathed.

Destiny is deeper than theology can explain. God does have a plan and a purpose for your life, but it is wrapped up in the very things you naturally enjoy, the things that give you a buzz. It is not something you constantly have to pray about. You don't need to go on a thirty-day fast to discover God's destiny for you. Enjoying life is not something to be ashamed of. So, the only real decision you have to make is whether to follow your dream, utilizing all the skills and abilities that God has blessed you with, or live a lifetime striving desperately to discover his purpose for your life.

God's number one plan for the world is that all people come to accept Jesus as their Lord and Saviour, and then live a life that is pleasing to God, as Jesus said: 'The one who sent me is with me; he has not left me alone, for I always do what pleases him' (John 8:29). We know Jesus did a good job of pleasing the Father because Scripture tells us so: when John the Baptist baptizes Jesus and then, during the transfiguration, when Jesus is seen talking with Moses and Elijah, the Father explicitly says that he is pleased with his Son.

What does it mean to live a life that is pleasing to God? In Luke 4:18–19, Jesus says he has come to bring freedom for all people – freedom from oppression, poverty and hunger. In this passage we see the heartbeat of God, which is to see burdens lifted and chains removed. He wants to see his people stand up against injustice, against violence, to bring peace instead of fear. God's primary characteristic is love, so pleasing God means bringing his love to everyone we come into contact with. He doesn't want a people that merely exist in the world, sitting impassively, waiting for Jesus to return, or for the moment when they are called to join him in heaven. God wants his people to be in a relationship with him and then to prosper, to lead nations, to lead in business. His heart is for his people to live life in abundance, and to live it now.

As a youngster, I noticed that the church often implicitly preached an anti-prosperity message, preferring instead to concentrate on a skewed idea of humility. The right kind of humility is a virtue we all need in our lives, but sometimes the church has unintentionally poured cold water on people's aspirations. In the well-known song, 'This Little Light of Mine' the emphasis is on 'little'. This kind of subconscious message discourages big dreams; it holds people back. Now is the time to start empowering people to live out their dreams. I want to encourage you to have confidence in who God made you to be, and in the dreams you have.

Peter Drucker, who was a writer and management consultant, said 'The best way to predict the future is to create it.' So, to what extent is our future predetermined? I believe God has a plan and a purpose for us (Jer. 29:11). However, God doesn't always tell us exactly where to go and what to do. We still need to choose to uncover the painting he has created on the canvas of our lives; whether we decide to do this is up to us. God has given us all we need for life and godliness, including wisdom and discernment. As you make decisions in life and follow the path that leads to fulfilling your dreams, ask yourself, 'Am I at peace with that decision?' The answer to that question will give you a useful indication as to whether you are following the right path. Sit and pray through some of the decisions you have made; sit in God's presence allowing his Spirit to minister to you. If the decisions are right, the peace of God will wash over you.

In Jeremiah 29:11 we are told that God's intention for our lives is peace and a future filled with hope. You simply need to live in the here and now, having fellowship with him every day, seeking first his kingdom. Tomorrow will take care of itself. Do this and you will see the hand of destiny on your life, even if this only becomes clear as you look back at what's happened – destiny is often revealed in hindsight. Like a racing car driver, keep your eyes on where you are going, keep your focus, or you may end up in the haystacks. Your true destiny is God-ordained. When you are living outside this destiny you may still achieve certain things, but it is only by allowing God to inhabit your dreams that you will start to see the results he intended for your life. As you get closer to God, your destiny will become clearer.

5

Trailblazers from The Word

And here I am today, eighty-five years old! I'm as strong
as I was the day Moses sent me out. I'm as strong as ever
in battle, whether coming or going. So give me this hill
country that God promised me.
Joshua 14:11,12, THE MESSAGE

The term 'trailblazer' resonates with me. I admire people who I think embody the word and I aspire to
demonstrate the qualities that the term suggests in my
own life. Trailblazers are true leaders, innovators and
pioneers in their calling. They don't simply replicate
what others are doing. They may make mistakes, but
they never quit. They have within them a spirit of self-
belief – in their dreams and in their destiny. They have a
passion and a reverence for the Word of God. God instils
his trailblazers with dreams and visions that change
lives.

In this chapter I want to look at biblical trailblazers.
The Bible is full of men and women who hold tight to a
God-inspired dream. God often uses them for a specific
purpose, although it is only in retrospect that we can see
how his plan unfolded, in many cases from the seeds of
very simple and personal dreams.

Jacob and Joseph

Joseph was the son of Jacob, who lived in Canaan, the land inherited by Abraham only a few years earlier. Jacob had many dreams and experiences that he no doubt shared with his children. He was a man who did almost anything to get a blessing: he deceived his father to get Isaac's blessing, and he wrestled with an angel until he received the promise of a blessing. Basically, he never gave up in his pursuit of the blessings of God.

His pioneer attitude and unquenchable pursuit of God would no doubt have been crystal clear to Jacob's children. I can imagine him at bedtime, recounting the story of the stairway to heaven, explaining to them how he wrestled with God, telling them with a deep passion how, in his dreams, he saw his descendants spreading across the earth and being a blessing to all nations. Imagine how his children, including Joseph, would have listened to his dream with awe and expectation. Being one of the youngest brothers, Joseph probably sat on his dad's knee as the dream was recounted every night. Is it any wonder that Joseph dreamed vividly?

Nowadays, barely a month goes by without a story in the news about a terrible massacre in a school or a violent street crime. Such incidents often prompt debate about what causes someone to act in such a cold-blooded way. Experts disagree about the level of influence exerted by popular culture – television, music, film, computer games – over the way someone behaves. But few would argue that the things we see and hear, both positive and negative, define the person we become.

If this is true, Jacob's experiences would have instilled in Joseph a firm sense of hope, and a belief that God was a God of blessing. It would have been clear to Joseph that his father was a dreamer, a man who pursued and received blessing after blessing.

The charismatic passion and the pioneer spirit exhibited by Jacob possibly shaped Joseph from an early age. Maybe he took the lead from his father's stories of blessing and became so affected by the passion rising in himself that it started to influence his dreams. The Scriptures tell us that 'Joseph had a dream' – not that 'God gave Joseph a dream'. In the same way that what we see and hear affects our dreams, the passion communicated by Jacob had a profound impact on Joseph's dreams. He started to recount the dreams to his brothers a long time before he had the necessary tools to handle the implications of what he was telling them. It's hardly surprising that Joseph walked around with his head held high, parading the technicolour coat. He had dreamed big and had an inkling of a destiny aligned with God's purposes.

In Genesis 37, Jacob commits to memory the dreams Joseph described. Perhaps he recognized in his son the same trailblazer spirit that he possessed:

> Joseph had a dream, and when he told it to his brothers, they hated him all the more. He said to them, 'Listen to this dream I had: We were binding sheaves of grain out in the field when suddenly my sheaf rose and stood upright, while your sheaves gathered around mine and bowed down to it.'
>
> His brothers said to him, 'Do you intend to reign over us? Will you actually rule us?' And they hated him all the more because of his dream and what he had said.
>
> Then he had another dream, and he told it to his brothers. 'Listen,' he said, 'I had another dream, and this time the sun and moon and eleven stars were bowing down to me.'
>
> When he told his father as well as his brothers, his father rebuked him and said, 'What is this dream you had? Will

your mother and I and your brothers actually come and bow down to the ground before you?' His brothers were jealous of him, but his father kept the matter in mind.

Gen. 37:5–11

Jacob was clearly a man who pursued God and he recognized that God was the source of all blessing. The dreams that Jacob, and ultimately Joseph, had were born out of an understanding of God and a life that pursued his presence.

The account of Joseph tells us that his brothers became so tired of his boasts that they dumped him in a well and then sold him into slavery. He ended up in prison, where he demonstrated God-given wisdom and the ability to interpret Pharaoh's dreams. He later became ruler of Egypt, in charge of distributing the grain, and ensuring that the country could survive the famine that swept the land. During the famine, his brothers went to Egypt for grain and ended up bowing down to Joseph. He later revealed himself to his brothers, thereby fulfilling the prophetic dream he had at seventeen.

What can we learn from Jacob and Joseph as trailblazers? Firstly, that neither man ever relented in the pursuit of his dreams. Secondly, that their dreams, in my opinion, were the result of an intimate relationship with God. Their dreams were not dictated by God, but were God-filled because of the personal relationship they had with him. Thirdly, that neither man was afraid of sharing his dreams, even when it meant scorn from the family. And, fourthly, in Joseph's case, that he was not equipped to deal with the scale of his dreams at first and he suffered for it. Pursuing and fulfilling our dreams may be a difficult, and certainly a character-building, process.

David

David was a shepherd boy who cared for his father's sheep in the fields around Bethlehem. We read in 1 Samuel 16 that he was anointed to be king, and lived with the knowledge he was chosen for many years without any inkling of how this could possibly become reality. We pick up the story in chapter seventeen at the time the Philistines were taunting the people of Israel on the battlefield. One day David's father asked him to take some food to his brothers at the battle camp. As David approached the camp, a dream that he could defeat the giant Goliath stirred inside him, but his brothers tried in vain to discourage and dispel his dream:

> When Eliab, David's oldest brother, heard him speaking with the men, he burned with anger at him and asked, 'Why have you come down here? And with whom did you leave those few sheep in the desert? I know how conceited you are and how wicked your heart is; you came down only to watch the battle'.
>
> 1 Sam. 17:28

With these words, his brother tried to belittle David. They reminded him of his mundane shepherding duties. He was told in no uncertain terms that he was destined for a life in the field, even though they were there when he was anointed to be King. Like Cinderella, he was told that his place was out of sight, away from the action. But, like Cinderella, he was not content with a future of mediocrity. David knew that God had more for him than that; he knew that God had chosen him to confront Goliath. With God's Word at the forefront of his mind, he faced the giant, defeated him and claimed victory for Israel over the Philistines:

You come against me with sword and spear and jav-
elin, but I come against you in the name of the LORD
Almighty, the God of the armies of Israel, whom you have
defied.

1 Sam. 17:45

David's dream to leave the field of sheep for the field of
battle came true. He made the right decisions that saw
him fulfil his destiny – a destiny that ultimately led to
him being crowned king of Israel. David was secure in
his future. He trusted in the Word of God and when the
time came to test that word in battle, God stood by him.
As the youngest in his family, David's brothers didn't
want him ruffling any feathers. It's safe to say he did
much more than that! He could so easily have listened to
his brothers and missed the destiny that was rightfully
his.

Abraham

Abraham had a simple dream. He longed for a son with
Sarah. But God had a much bigger plan than to give them
a child. He wanted to bless Abraham, but his vision was
for a whole nation to be born. Abraham and his son, Isaac,
gave way to the fulfilment of that promise and the occu-
pation of Canaan. Because of Abraham's faith in God, he
pursued his dreams. He didn't know it, but his dreams
were intertwined with God's plan:

By faith Abraham, when called to go to a place he would
later receive as his inheritance, obeyed and went, even
though he did not know where he was going.

Heb. 11:8

Nehemiah

The account of Nehemiah is often used to help aspiring leaders. He oversaw the rebuilding of the walls around Jerusalem, and we can learn a lot from his leadership in the account of how he undertook the process. But I want to look at why Nehemiah rebuilt Jerusalem's walls. After all, we know he lived over a thousand miles away in Babylon. He wasn't a free man and he wasn't even a builder by trade. What motivated him?

Effectively the rebuilding of Jerusalem's walls was the rebuilding of a broken dream – someone else's broken dream. Nehemiah didn't conceive the original dream, but he took it upon himself to rebuild it.

Jerusalem had fallen into disrepair 140 years before Nehemiah was even born. That's a long time for a dream to die:

The words of Nehemiah son of Hacaliah:

In the month of Kislev in the twentieth year, while I was in the citadel of Susa, Hanani, one of my brothers, came from Judah with some other men, and I questioned them about the Jewish remnant that survived the exile, and also about Jerusalem.

They said to me, 'Those who survived the exile and are back in the province are in great trouble and disgrace. The wall of Jerusalem is broken down, and its gates have been burned with fire.'

When I heard these things, I sat down and wept. For some days I mourned and fasted and prayed before the God of heaven. Then I said:

'O LORD, God of heaven, the great and awesome God, who keeps his covenant of love with those who love him and obey his commands, let your ear be attentive and your eyes open to hear the prayer your servant is praying before you day and night for your servants, the people of Israel. I confess the sins we Israelites, including myself and my father's house, have committed against you. We have acted very wickedly toward you. We have not obeyed the commands, decrees and laws you gave your servant Moses.

'Remember the instruction you gave your servant Moses, saying, "If you are unfaithful, I will scatter you among the nations, but if you return to me and obey my commands, then even if your exiled people are at the farthest horizon, I will gather them from there and bring them to the place I have chosen as a dwelling for my Name."

They are your servants and your people, whom you redeemed by your great strength and your mighty hand. O LORD, let your ear be attentive to the prayer of this your servant and to the prayer of your servants who delight in revering your Name. Give your servant success today by granting him favour in the presence of this man.'

I was cupbearer to the king.

Neh. 1

Nehemiah's prayer reveals the man behind the dream. It is clear from the start that Nehemiah had a fantastic relationship with God. He lived with an overwhelming conviction of God's providence. He fasted and prayed diligently after he heard about the state of Jerusalem. As a servant to the king of Persia, he also recognized himself as a servant of God. Through this close and intimate relationship with God, he had a dream that, to outsiders, would appear impossible. As Nehemiah so boldly confesses in his prayer, however, God is God of his promises, and therefore the seemingly impossible can be made possible. Impossible can be just a word that people use as an excuse not to try something new. But if we tap into the promises God has made, things can happen. God had made a covenant with Moses, so it was without hesitation that Nehemiah stepped out in faith, believing God is unchanging and that what he did for Moses, he could do for him.

Nehemiah asked God to give him success, specifically when he approached the King of Persia to ask for permission to go to Jerusalem. The King granted permission and Nehemiah recognized that this was because of the favour of God.

There were probably thousands of people who saw Jerusalem in ruins on a daily basis, but no one actually made a commitment to do anything about it. Nehemiah was a cupbearer by trade. He had no building experience. But his spirit was aggrieved and he was motivated to do something to change the situation.

Reading chapters one to six of the book of Nehemiah, we learn of all the different obstacles that Nehemiah had to overcome in the pursuit of his dream. Not only was he a great starter, but more importantly, he was also a finisher. He formulated a plan to realize his dream, and with this plan he overcame every obstacle. He recognized that relationships with other people were a key factor in his success, and gathered good people around him to assist him. Miracles begin with a relationship – first a relationship with God, and then relationships with others. Too many times people try to exercise faith without nurturing their relationship with God. Nehemiah knew his dream would remain buried in the rubble unless he recognized God and developed relationships with others. Nehemiah did not quit until his dream became a reality.

New Direction

A lot of our heroes of faith started on one track in life only to come up against roadblocks, which forced them in a new direction. Having been diverted, they simply pursued the new path with as much zeal and passion. Saul had an encounter with Jesus on the road to Damascus. He was heading one way, but ended up going in another. From building tents, he went on to become the architect of the church. Ruth was orphaned at an early age, and she and her mother-in-law lost their husbands. This catalogue of disasters would normally have resulted in them being ostracized from society. But God had another plan: Ruth became the great-grandmother of King David. Who would have imagined that this would be possible – except the God of the impossible?

6

Journey of Life

The centre of every man's existence is a dream. Death, disease, insanity, are merely material accidents, like a toothache or a twisted ankle. That these brutal forces always besiege and often capture the citadel does not prove that they are the citadel.
G.K. Chesterton

G.K. Chesterton was a famous author and journalist during the First World War and was well known in the field of Christian apologetics. The quote above succinctly describes the journey of every man and woman. As we go through life, we are besieged by different challenges that can chip away at our dreams.

Every age and every stage of life brings another trial. These challenges may encourage us to give up. As we get older and maybe have children, with all the associated responsibilities that family life brings, it is easy to accept the mediocre status quo. A lot of people stop dreaming, accepting their place in life, grumbling about what they don't have or resenting people who appear to have made it in the world.

If you are able to resist the temptation to quit, at some point you will have a breakthrough. We live in an era where age is no longer a barrier to accomplishing dreams. Have you given up on a dream because you think you are past it? Just look at Duncan Bannatyne, the Scottish entrepreneur who is one of the panel of business people on the BBC's *Dragon's Den*. His success came late in life, after he started in business at the age of thirty as an ice-cream man. In his book *Anyone Can Do It* he explains that he was determined not to be poor. Asked if anyone could really make a million, he answered that so many people talk about how it's not fair they don't have any money when they themselves could do something to bring about change. I'm not saying that everyone's dream is related to money. As I said before, some people dream of seeing families restored, to go on an exotic holiday, or move to a nicer area. Often we are restricted in the pursuit of our dreams due to sickness, or other environmental or economic circumstances. I simply want to encourage you to pursue the dream you have and, like Duncan Bannatyne, do all you can to make it happen.

If you ask my four-year-old daughter what she wants to do when she's older, she will tell you that she doesn't want to grow up, that she wants to stay young and always be with mummy and daddy. Her life naturally revolves around ours, and her experience of life is therefore very limited. As she starts school her experiences will grow, her life will develop and she will start having aspirations and dreams about her future that match her talents and passions. But, even as a four-year-old, I want to encourage her to dream, to tell me what she wants to do. She may or may not keep those dreams close to her heart and continue to pursue them later in life. What matters is that she knows from a young age what it's like to dream.

When I was fifteen years old, one of my dreams was to run a hotel. My dad, as a local council health inspector, had good connections with hotels in the city of Leeds and arranged two weeks of work experience for me at one of them. I will always remember this dream because I recorded it in my journal. I wrote down all the things I believed I would need in a hotel, from the bed linen to the kitchen utensils. I kept this journal because, naïvely, I thought I could turn my dream into reality almost immediately. Within a year the dream had become dormant and it stayed that way for a long time, despite the fact that I went on to work for one of the largest hotel chains in the UK and then as a Global Supply Chain Director, supplying hotels with various technologies.

The dream stirred again when I was thirty-three, when I asked my church pastor to pray for me. Without having any idea about the dream I had held as a teenager, he described a vision of me owning hotels across the world. Not only had I never told him about my dream, but I had completely forgotten about it myself. However, something inside me recognized that this prayer was significant. I acted almost immediately and took some time out to look at nearly every hotel for sale. I found a rather nice sixty-bedroom, pastel-coloured, art deco hotel. I took down all the agent's details and emailed requesting more information. It transpired that this particular hotel was on the market for more than $12m and required a thirty per cent down payment. It was way beyond my means, but at least I had rekindled the dream. Like Joseph, Jacob's son, I was talking about my dreams before I had developed the integrity and character to turn them into reality.

I mention this because, at this moment in my life, the dream seems further away than ever. I have a mortgage to pay and a family to feed, but I believe God is a God of the miraculous and I continue to hold on to the dream. I will not quit. I feel like Caleb, from the book of Joshua who, at the age of forty, was sent by Moses to spy on the Promised Land. During this trip, Caleb conceived a new dream that remained with him for another forty-five years:

> Now the men of Judah approached Joshua at Gilgal, and Caleb son of Jephunneh the Kenizzite said to him, 'You know what the LORD said to Moses the man of God at Kadesh Barnea about you and me. I was forty years old when Moses the servant of the LORD sent me from Kadesh Barnea to explore the land. And I brought him back a report according to my convictions, but my brothers who went up with me made the hearts of the people melt with fear. I, however, followed the LORD my God wholeheartedly. So on that day Moses swore to me, "The land on which your feet have walked will be your inheritance and that of your children forever, because you have followed the LORD my God wholeheartedly."
>
> 'Now then, just as the LORD promised, he has kept me alive for forty-five years since the time he said this to Moses, while Israel moved about in the desert. So here I am today, eighty-five years old! I am still as strong today as the day Moses sent me out; I'm just as vigorous to go out to battle now as I was then. Now give me this hill country that the LORD promised me that day.
>
> Josh. 14:6–12

Caleb had to wait over forty-five years before his dream became a reality. Throughout that time he maintained his strength and his convictions, he didn't relent, he kept hold of his dream. I just can't get over the fact that this eighty-five-year-old was able to say, 'I am stronger now than back then. Give me my mountain!' I am so inspired by Caleb that I hope when I am eighty-five years old I can say, 'Give me my hotel.'

As we journey through life, we often experience delays in the fulfilment of our dreams. Forty-five years seems a long time for a dream to be fulfilled, but remember, Joseph also had to wait. He was even sold as a slave and put in prison – what a test of the faith that must have been! He must have gone through times when he doubted his dream would ever become a reality. So, too, Lazarus, who was dead for three days before Jesus told him to come out of the tomb (John 11).

It is easy to become impatient, to believe that the fulfilment of a dream should be instantaneous, but God has a plan that we simply cannot fathom. What seems like a hold-up to us is actually a divine delay. The difference between the two is in our perspective. From the throne room of heaven everything is on time, everything is on schedule. God sees the mountain being given to Caleb at eighty-five, but he also sees the character being formed in the Israelites as they go through the desert. God sees Lazarus rising from the dead, but he also sees the greater glory being poured out. God has a timeline that is very different from ours. When we have a dream or vision we expect instant fulfillment, but as in the case of Lazarus, God's timing is very different. What would you say to the people waiting around Lazarus' tomb waiting for Jesus to arrive?

We simply cannot comprehend why some dreams are fulfilled and some not, but our trust must be in God and in his faithfulness. We just need to believe. As with Caleb, we must follow Jesus wholeheartedly all the days of our life, regardless of what we see with our own eyes. As Paul in writing to the Corinthians says, we must walk by faith and not by sight:

For we walk by faith [we regulate our lives and conduct ourselves by our conviction or belief respecting man's relationship to God and divine things, with trust and holy fervour; thus we walk] not by sight or appearance.

2 Cor. 5:7, AMP

This principle is perhaps most recently demonstrated in the life of the famous Bradford evangelist Smith Wigglesworth, who often went around telling hearers to simply believe, have faith, and not be ruled by what they saw or heard.

7

Character

Character is like a tree and reputation like a shadow. The shadow is what we think of it; the tree is the real thing.
Abraham Lincoln

In a world where, increasingly, anything goes, moral strength of character is an unfashionable notion. To appear open-minded to any lifestyle choice, any way of behaving, is considered liberal. Questioning the way someone conducts themselves is an antiquated idea, likely to see you branded orthodox, unadventurous, conservative, even anti-social or dangerous. To some extent there is now no distinction between right and wrong.

This sense of amorality has begun to filter through to the church, sometimes explicitly and sometimes behind closed doors. Godly character is hard to find. A recent study by a well-known hotel chain in America showed that when a particular annual Christian convention comes to town, use of adult channels in its hotel rooms increases. Good godly character has been thrown out the window even, in some cases, by the church itself.

Problems occur in a church setting when too much emphasis is placed on an individual's gifting. Talent can be confused for godliness. A skilful guitarist does not necessarily make a good worship leader. A powerful orator is not the same thing as an anointed preacher. Putting the wrong person in a position of authority can have a damaging impact on the people for whom they are responsible. How many times have supposed moves of God come to an abrupt end because of a major character flaw in those at the forefront of a ministry? God doesn't change, the song may well be God-inspired, the message just as powerful, the move of God no less real, but human imperfection can have a prematurely weakening effect.

A desire for God's anointing must be allied to our own willingness to build godly character. Without it, the anointing will soon dwindle. The message in many churches – that heaven is waiting to rain down on us, to anoint us – is true in one sense. However, the Bible explicitly tells us that it is what flows out of us that God is interested in:

> He who believes in Me [who cleaves to and trusts in and relies on Me] as the Scripture has said, From his innermost being shall flow [continuously] springs and rivers of living water.
>
> John 7:38, AMP

This is a picture of heaven flowing through our core being. I can fall to the ground because of the power of the Holy Spirit every day, but unless my core being, my core character, is changed, then all I am doing is getting a bad back from hitting the floor.

We need to rediscover what it means to be a Christian again, what it means to display godly character, what it means to be a man or a woman of God. I believe we are often afraid to talk about character because we are aware of character flaws in our own lives. Matthew seven is often used to reinforce the idea that we must not question someone's character:

> Do not judge, or you too will be judged. For in the same way you judge others, you will be judged, and with the measure you use, it will be measured to you.
>
> Why do you look at the speck of sawdust in your brother's eye and pay no attention to the plank in your own eye? How can you say to your brother, 'Let me take the speck out of your eye,' when all the time there is a plank in your own eye? You hypocrite, first take the plank out of your own eye, and then you will see clearly to remove the speck from your brother's eye.
>
> Do not give dogs what is sacred; do not throw your pearls to pigs. If you do, they may trample them under their feet, and then turn and tear you to pieces.
>
> Matt. 7:1–6

We all have character flaws, or aspects of our private lives that we are working on, but that shouldn't prevent us from helping one another to develop, in love. By being accountable ourselves and by discipling others, we can hone the character traits that Jesus perfected. It is vitally important to allow people we can trust to identify characteristics in us that need work.

Without godly character, we might still successfully pursue a dream of seeing a school in Kenya established, of writing the book we always believed we could, of composing the worship song that has been simmering inside us. But, invariably, the success will be short-lived because we are not strong enough to sustain it. We cannot afford to ignore character development.

Traditionally, those in positions of authority were looked up to as examples of good character. Teachers were model citizens; there was respect for police, fire and ambulance personnel. A person of good character was someone to be admired and respected. Children were given positive moral grounding in movements like the Scouts. Robert Baden-Powell, the founder of the Scouts, aimed to provide some of the spirit of self-negation, self-discipline, sense of humour, responsibility, helpfulness to others, loyalty and patriotism which go to make 'character'. He described his movement as nothing less than a 'character factory'.

What Is Character?

Character, as defined by Dr Creflo Dollar in his book *8 Steps To Create the Life You Want*, can be interpreted simply as 'doing the right thing'.[3] Our personal character will often be reflected in the way we handle situations or circumstances that we face every day. To refer to Cinderella, in the midst of hardship she held her head high and kept her dream close. By contrast, her stepmother's bad attitude was reflected in the way she treated Cinderella.

Character is what results in one person doing right and another person doing wrong. Doing the wrong thing is often far easier than doing right. On a basic level, it might be easier to give in to a child's demands for sweets for the sake of a quiet life, than to continue to refuse them because we know it would be bad for them. Under peer pressure, it might be easier to agree to that extra beer, even though you know it will be one too many. It's often easier to say 'yes' than to say 'no'.

However, as Christians our standards should be set by the Word of God and our understanding of it should dictate how we behave. The Bible is clear about how our character ought to be. Paul sums up character in Galatians five; he calls it the fruit of the Spirit:

> The acts of the sinful nature are obvious: sexual immorality, impurity and debauchery; idolatry and witchcraft; hatred, discord, jealousy, fits of rage, selfish ambition, dissensions, factions and envy; drunkenness, orgies, and the like. I warn you, as I did before, that those who live like this will not inherit the kingdom of God.
>
> But the fruit of the Spirit is love, joy, peace, patience, kindness, goodness, faithfulness, gentleness and self-control. Against such things there is no law. Those who belong to Christ Jesus have crucified the sinful nature with its passions and desires. Since we live by the Spirit, let us keep in step with the Spirit. Let us not become conceited, provoking and envying each other.
>
> Gal. 5:19–26

As Christians we need to be a people who live in peace with one another. We must be kind. We should be faithful in the things we do and the things we are responsible for. In all things we need to show self-control and gentleness. This fruit of the Spirit is not handed to us on a plate, but it lives in us and becomes more pronounced as we stay close to God and allow his Word to change us. We need to start displaying our godly conscience at work and in our play, to show godly morality in our business dealings and godly principles in our pursuit of science. We need godly character.

Love is God's primary characteristic and the number one character trait exhibited by Jesus. Without love we can't do anything. However, I want to look at some other characteristics that are easy to ignore in a society that may deem them old-fashioned: self-discipline and righteous behaviour.

Self-Discipline

Success in any field – sports, the arts, academia – requires practise. Practise requires self-discipline; the self-discipline to get up at five a.m. to train in the rain when we would rather stay in bed, to rehearse that line of the script until it's branded on our memory, to stay in the library to read every last page of that heavyweight textbook when the sun is shining outside.

Well-known Christian author Rick Joyner has written a number of study guides, one of which is called *Fifty Days for a Soaring Vision*. His theory is that it takes fifty days to form habits in our lives. To develop a godly habit takes self-discipline but, once it becomes routine, it governs how we behave and reflects the godly character that we are developing. Ultimately, the level of self-discipline we commit to will determine whether we achieve our dreams.

Dr Dollar puts forward a model that outlines a process for achieving destiny. It's what I call the 'supply-chain of success'. The process starts with a seed, God's Word, and culminates with the realization of destiny. I have summarized the eight steps he describes in his book:

1. God's Word changes our thinking
2. Our thinking affects our emotions
3. Our changed emotions help us make more powerful decisions
4. Our decisions alter our actions
5. Our actions establish healthy habits
6. Our habits develop godly character
7. Our changed character will affect our ultimate destiny
8. Our destiny can be embraced

The foundation of the entire process is self-discipline. It requires self-discipline to plant diligently the seed of the Word of God in your heart, to allow it to change your thinking, your emotions, your decisions, your habits and your character. It is not easy – you will find yourself swimming against the current and refusing to accept what the world tells you is right, what is acceptable. It takes self-discipline and strength of character to stand by your decisions, but the reward for your steadfastness in this respect will be godly character and success in the pursuit of your dreams.

Righteous Behaviour

I will always remember my 17th birthday. It is etched on my memory for life. I went to the local pub with some friends who, as a practical joke, spiked a couple of the soft drinks I had ordered. We left at closing time and on the way home, I started messing around, hiding behind bushes and jumping out at my friends. It was all a bit of a laugh until, to my shock, I saw my church pastor across the road. At the time I lived in a small village and my church was over twelve miles away. The pastor lived in another area altogether and the chances of him being on that street at eleven p.m. on a Friday night were miniscule – so much so that I thought I was hallucinating!

It all became very real, however, when at church the following Sunday, he pulled my parents to one side and later called me for a meeting. He simply asked me, 'Was that any way for you to behave as a Christian?' I felt hard done by. My drinks had been spiked and I hadn't intentionally gone out to get drunk. But the memory has stayed with me for the last fifteen years, and I believe I was fortunate to have had the experience of being pulled up by the pastor at seventeen. It was an early lesson. I firmly believe that our conduct should always be consistent with the Word, and how Jesus behaved. We need to treat our bodies as temples of the Holy Spirit. Ask yourself: what would Jesus do? Would he get drunk? Would he smoke? Would he swear? Would he do his best at work and play?

Asking yourself what you are really like when the doors are shut and no one else is around can be an acid test. When you are on business and staying in a hotel, what channels are you watching? Do you take the clothes hangers or the towels home? When you go to the supermarket and are handed extra change, do you give it straight back? If you knew you would never be found out, what would you do? These things might sound insignificant, but they reflect the righteousness of our characters.

How would you react if you lost your job? Our identities are very much tied up with what we do for a living. Being deprived of that can make us feel unsure of who we are, which in turn can make us resentful, self-critical and depressed. But your character goes further than simply the job you do. When I lost my main source of income, my friends commented on how strong I was. The fact of the matter was that I was able to keep faith in my future because I kept the Word of God close.

Your character is integral to achieving your dreams. Dr Dollar tells us that we will never rise above the limitations of our character. He is right. Our dreams will never come true if our character is not aligned with the magnitude of the dream. Before dreams can be fulfilled, we must develop the right character to meet the dream.

Joseph's dream came to him before his character was able to carry it. He tried to share the dream with his family and then walk in it, but failed. His brothers became jealous of him and he was thrown in a pit. I often wonder what would have happened if Joseph hadn't bragged to his brothers before his character was mature enough to handle the dream. I'm sure God would have guided him to his destiny and his brothers would still have bowed down to him. But perhaps he would have maintained a relationship with them throughout. Perhaps there was no reason for him to have lost those years in jail. In my opinion it was his lack of character in his formative years that meant he was unable to carry the dream. As time went on, his character caught up, events unfolded, and the dream became reality.

8

You Can Achieve Your Dreams

All men dream, but not equally. Those who dream by
night in the dusty recesses of their minds wake in the day
to find that it was vanity; but the dreamers of the day are
dangerous men, for they may act their dream with open
eyes, to make it possible.
T.E. Lawrence

Millions of young men died on the battlefields of Europe
and beyond during the First and Second World Wars, and
with them millions of embryonic dreams died too. Those
young men were robbed of the chance to chase their
dreams.

Every day, countless numbers of other dreams die
because of unfulfilled aspirations; dreams that fall victim
to self-doubt, self-criticism, or simply the constraints of
time and daily responsibility. This is a tragedy. I want to
encourage you to press forward to achieve your dream.
Don't quit, don't get discouraged, keep going. Your
dream is alive – so embrace the opportunity to keep
going.

Over the next couple of chapters, I want to move from
the theoretical 'why' to the practical 'how' of achieving
our dreams. Our future is in our hands. What I mean by

this is that God has a destiny for us, a painting that is waiting to be uncovered, but we have to choose to get involved. There is no magic formula, but God has given us all the gifts and abilities we need. It's time to put our faith into action. Having a dream is all very well, but if we do nothing practical to help it happen then nothing *will* happen. If you have a dream to be an evangelist, to tell people about Jesus, you need to leave the house, and actually go out and meet people, so that your dream can be achieved.

I want to share some practical steps that will give you the best chance of success.

Keep Your Dream in Mind at All Times

I have a friend who has a dream of giving £1m to his church. This dream probably sounds far-fetched, but his levels of faith are as big as his dream. To keep his dream ever-present, he has actually written the £1m cheque and stuck it to his fridge. Every time he goes to get some milk, the dream is staring him in the face, a constant reminder of the target he has set himself. He knows that to achieve his dream his faith needs to keep rising.

In a similar way, I have a scrapbook containing pictures of hotels and locations that I have cut out of magazines as a visual way of keeping my hotel-chain dream in mind. I have signed up to estate agents and investors' databases, which send me regular emails with details of hotels for sale.

If you have a dream of owning a particular car, go and take a test drive, even if you know you can't afford it today. If you fantasize about becoming a pilot, take regular trips to the small airfields and get acquainted with other pilots. If you have a dream to build a school in

Kenya, get in touch with mission agencies working in the area and sign up to their newsletters. It may seem like the dream is a million miles away. But, as Confucius said, 'A journey of a thousand miles begins with a single step.' There may be a million small steps to take before you achieve your dream and you need to get practical, now. Your dream won't just materialize out of thin air. Take the first practical step and you will notice that God will start to bless you supernaturally.

Be a Good Steward of Money

In the Gospel of Matthew, there is an account of the parable of the talents that Jesus told as an illustration of the kingdom of heaven:

> Again, it will be like a man going on a journey, who called his servants and entrusted his property to them. To one he gave five talents of money, to another two talents, and to another one talent, each according to his ability. Then he went on his journey. The man who had received the five talents went at once and put his money to work and gained five more. So also, the one with the two talents gained two more. But the man who had received the one talent went off, dug a hole in the ground and hid his master's money.
>
> After a long time the master of those servants returned and settled accounts with them. The man who had received the five talents brought the other five. 'Master,' he said, 'you entrusted me with five talents. See, I have gained five more.' His master replied, 'Well done, good and faithful servant! You have been faithful with a few things; I will put you in charge of many things. Come and share your master's happiness!'

The man with the two talents also came. 'Master,' he said, 'you entrusted me with two talents; see, I have gained two more.'

His master replied, 'Well done, good and faithful servant! You have been faithful with a few things; I will put you in charge of many things. Come and share your master's happiness!'

Then the man who had received the one talent came. 'Master,' he said, 'I knew that you are a hard man, harvesting where you have not sown and gathering where you have not scattered seed. So I was afraid and went out and hid your talent in the ground. See, here is what belongs to you.' His master replied, 'You wicked, lazy servant! So you knew that I harvest where I have not sown and gather where I have not scattered seed? Well then, you should have put my money on deposit with the bankers, so that when I returned I would have received it back with interest.

'Take the talent from him and give it to the one who has the ten talents. For everyone who has will be given more, and he will have an abundance. Whoever does not have, even what he has will be taken from him. And throw that worthless servant outside, into the darkness, where there will be weeping and gnashing of teeth'.

Matt. 25:14–30

This parable provides an important message about the wise management of our finances. It is all very well asking God, 'Why aren't you blessing me?' But if you blow all your disposable income on material possessions, why should he be expected to entrust you with the greater responsibility that comes with greater financial wealth?

We live in a world of instant coffee, ready meals, drive-through takeaways, drive-in laundry and, in some countries, even drive-in weddings. Corners are constantly being cut so that we can get what we want, fast. We have become too busy to grind the coffee beans ourselves, to sit and eat the food in the restaurant – even, apparently, to get out of the car to say, 'I do.' When we see something we want, credit allows us to get it even if we don't have the money in our bank accounts. We have increasingly come to expect instant results.

There's the same temptation with our dreams. We want to see them realized immediately rather than looking at the steps it will take to achieve them. This kind of mentality has infiltrated the church. I've heard people say things like, 'Name it and claim it', or 'Blab it and grab it'. In the sense that we are able to lay claim to the things that God has promised, there is some truth in these slogans but we also need to understand that there is a process involved that will form good habits in us, and habits will take us further in life than a simple wish list. The process that builds a habit will give you the character you need to enable you to handle the success of the dream longer than an instant win. You only need to look at how many lottery millionaires lose it all very quickly or cannot handle their new wealth to see that an instant win is not necessarily a good thing.

God himself could have created the world in a day, but he took six. He understands the importance of process.

9

Tools to Achieve Your Dreams
Part One: Get Your Thinking
Right

An inconvenience is only an adventure wrongly considered; an adventure is an inconvenience rightly considered.
G.K. Chesterton

If we have invited Jesus to be our Lord and Saviour, we
have the innate ability not only to achieve our dreams,
hopes and desires, but to do much more than we dare
imagine. We have what it takes to be a success every
moment of the day. Luck and fate have nothing to do with
it:

Now to Him who, by . . . the . . . power that is at work within us, is able to . . . do superabundantly, far over and above
all that we . . . ask or think [infinitely beyond our highest
prayers, desires, thoughts, hopes, or dreams] – To Him be
glory in the church and in Christ Jesus throughout all generations forever and ever. Amen.

Eph. 3:20,21, AMP

It is one thing simply to read this Scripture, but entirely another to allow it to change our lives. Simply reading the Word and learning it by rote will not change us. We must move from merely knowing, in a detached way, the truths of the Word, to a full and complete understanding of what they mean so that the Word may alter our entire way of thinking and, ultimately, the everyday decision-making that empowers us to fulfil our dreams. The road to success starts in a mind that has been reprogrammed with God's Word. This chapter will look at some ways you can start to change your thought process, and the next chapter will go through some practical steps to bring you closer to fulfilment.

Get Into the Word

There are a few Christian TV programmes that really dishonour the Word of God by encouraging viewers to call premium rate numbers to receive a so-called instant prophetic word. If the callers were grounded in the Word of God and had an understanding of its simple truths they would see this for what it is – a cold, calculated, money-spinning gimmick. We need a solid footing in the Word of God if we are to achieve our dreams. In an age in which we are constantly bombarded with messages in instant form, from radio and television to podcasts and blogs, it is easy to be led astray by wishy-washy doctrine and theology. Like a ship on the ocean, we can be tossed around on waves of conflicting ideology if we have no personal conviction, grounded in the Word of God. This is why we need to be careful about the people we listen to, the music we listen to, which preachers we follow, which podcasts we download, which books we read and which church we attend. Always consider who is doing the feeding in your life.

The most important thing is to start regularly getting into the Word of God. If you are not grounded in the Word, you will be shaken when confronted with a challenge. If you are pursuing a dream and face a major crisis, you will be shaken off course. In order to be strong in your convictions and in your knowledge and understanding, you need to get into the Word. Do you meditate on the Word? If you don't know how to meditate, ask yourself: do you worry? Worry is simply negative meditation. It's dwelling on things that are troubling you.

Meditating on the Word is reading a Scripture and keeping it on your mind, ready to use. If you imagine the Word of God as a seed, then you can picture how that seed needs to settle in your heart and be watered and nurtured as it grows. If you allow God's Word to root itself in your very being, you will start to see major changes in your life. It will affect your health, your wellbeing, your relationships, your finances. God's Word never returns void and empty. He has given us everything we need in the Word to be a success. So it's with confidence that you can say, 'I can do all things, I can overcome every obstacle that gets in the way, because it is written in the Word'. You will start to gain a complete understanding of God and what you can achieve by living as a Christian.

It's this complete understanding that is often missing in people's lives. They are able to read the Bible and know superficially that Jesus died on the cross and rose again, and that they are saved. But there is more to being a Christian than just being saved. We all need to graduate from a childish understanding of the Word to a mature grasp of the truths that are key to living a successful life. In Colossians 1:9, Paul says that he is praying that they, the people of Colossae, would gain a complete under-standing of what God wants to do in their lives. In verse 10, he goes on to say that this was in order that they might live for God and please him in every way. This message is the same for us. As we read, meditate on, and allow the Word of God to transform us, we will start to gain a com-plete understanding. It's basically moving from having knowledge, to gaining wisdom. The difference is often simply the application of knowledge into our lives. Then we will live a life worthy of the Lord and please him in every way.

A friend of mine gave me a great analogy of the differ-ence between knowledge and wisdom: knowledge is knowing that a tomato is a fruit. Wisdom is knowing not to put the tomato in a fruit salad.

Get Rid of the Language of Unbelief

As you read the Word and see how God promises to bless people that believe in him, your faith levels will increase. You will start to walk in the dreams that you have fostered. Your mind will be anchored in the hope of what God has said in his Word. In order to stay anchored and focused in pursuit of your dreams, you need to guard the words that come out of your mouth and the words that you listen to. Never allow someone else to destroy your dreams through what they say. The saying 'sticks and stones may break my bones, but words can never hurt me' is a fallacy. Words can really damage a dream and destroy a life:

If anyone speaks, he should do it as one speaking the very words of God.

1 Pet. 4:11

Have you noticed how economic recessions can snowball as more and more people talk about house prices, mortgages and interest rates? If you believe you are in a personal recession, it will become a self-fulfilling prophecy. If you start talking about losing your job, expect to see that coming. You need to stop talking negatively, even if everything you see is negative. Start talking about increase, about achieving your dream, because you can. God has increase on his mind, not failure. You need to start thinking about increase and stop talking the language of unbelief.

Get Your Thinking Right

Avoid watching or reading things that will compromise your thoughts and dilute your resolve. Your thinking is the catalyst for your actions and habits and will, ultimately, determine whether or not you achieve your dreams. To realize your dreams, keep your mind pure.

Dreams are the product of our mindset. If you say to a four-year-old, 'Never run into the road without looking' they will envision what it would be like to run into the road, and their motivation for not doing so is born out of fear. If instead you say to them, 'Always stand and hold my hand while we cross the road' the child will imagine what it is like to stand with their hand in yours at the roadside, and their motivation is more of a positive one, linked to feelings of love and security. In the same way, our thinking needs to align itself with the Word so that we don't run off across the road but hold onto our Father's hand. We must capture every thought and bring it into obedience with Christ (2 Cor. 10:5). We must meditate on pure thoughts and the truth:

Finally, brothers, whatever is true, whatever is noble, whatever is right, whatever is pure, whatever is lovely, whatever is admirable – if anything is excellent or praiseworthy – think about such things.

Phil. 4:8

Set your mind on the things above. When a wrong thought comes into your mind, capture it and replace it with the truth from the Word. That's what Jesus did when he was tempted for forty days and nights in the desert. Every lie that the devil told him, he counter-attacked with the Word of truth.

Don't Allow Critics to Distract You

You may be tempted to give up on your dream by the first person that comes along with a strong opinion. Be ready for criticism: anyone who pursues a dream and who starts to draw attention to themselves because they are doing something extraordinary will inevitably find themselves being analyzed. Criticism is often a sign that you are doing something right. You don't need to please your critics, and not everyone will understand your dream. Don't allow them to hold you back. If you allow your critics to poison your dream, you will end up settling for less. When Joseph's brothers rejected him and sold him into slavery, he didn't become bitter, he didn't blame God or start scheming to get his own back. He kept the dream in his heart and allowed time to prove him right.

Discipleship: Teach and Be Teachable

Companies will only invest time in and give added responsibility to someone who is teachable. If you want to release your potential and achieve your dreams, you need to be someone who can be taught. Arrogance and conceit will have the opposite effect. A teachable person needs humility, needs to listen. It can be the hardest thing to accept, but it is a vital attribute if you are going to learn and move forward.

As a disciple, you may be told things which are difficult to accept, and it is easy to get defensive. Your teacher may identify things in your life that need to change if you are to attain your dream. They may identify fruitless things that are sapping your energies and other things that you need to refocus on. Like the tree being pruned, there may be aspects of your life that need to be cut back. It can be a painful process, but in the end it will mean that you are better able to bear fruit.

Build Yourself Up with Truth

Having the right perception of yourself is important. You need to know what God has done in you and who you are in Christ. It might seem like a strange example, but I love the film *Cool Runnings*, about the Jamaican bobsled team that went to the 1988 Winter Olympics. The idea that a group of Caribbean island boys could compete in such an event seems ridiculous at face value. But they had a dream and they pursued it.

One of the film's main characters is Junior Bevill, a rich boy whose dream it is to compete. His dad has other ideas and, when Junior finally makes it, his dad turns up unannounced at the Olympic village to bring him home. The confrontation leaves Junior unsettled. He desperately wants to realize his dream, but the pressure brought to bear by his father and the doubt he has in himself cause him to waver. Then another member of the bobsled team, Yul Brenner, gives him a pep talk:

> Yul: Look in the mirror, and tell me what you see!
> Junior: I see Junior.
> Yul: You see Junior? Well, let me tell you what I see. I see pride! I see power! I see a badass mother who don't take any crap off nobody![4]

Yul reminds Junior how strong he is and what he believes in. I'm not sure anyone has ever drawn parallels between *Cool Runnings* and the Old Testament before, but it reminds me of Moses repeatedly telling the Israelites to 'be strong and courageous' in Deuteronomy thirty-one.

We need to remember God's opinion of us, not our own. Tell yourself out loud who you are in Christ: 'I can do all things through Christ who strengthens me, there is nothing at all that God cannot do and that goes the same for me. I have the same Spirit that raised Christ from the dead. Christ lives in me, the hope, the glory in me!' Every day, as you wake up, declare to the Lord that you are depending on him today, and not on your own resources, position, power or talents. This declaration effectively leaves him in charge of you and the day's activities.

Spiritual Authority

It is easy to blame God for the bad things that happen in our lives, but we need to know God doesn't cause these things. The thief, that is the devil, comes to steal, kill and destroy (John 10:10). God has given us authority over the devil, and it's really up to us to take that authority and command the devil to flee. If we don't do anything about it, then nothing will happen! We need to walk in that authority. We are the prophets of our own lives. If we aren't seeing things happen, we have the God-given authority to speak prophetically into our own lives. Use the authority to speak against negative thinking. Stand in the Word of God, rebuke what is false and bring it into alignment with God's Word. Things will not change if we idly sit back and say, 'It must be the Lord's will that I go through this.' It plainly says in the Word what the will of God is, so take a look at it. It's not the will of God for marriages to break up, for you to be in debt, for you to lose a job or to die of sickness. We live in a fallen world where things like this happen all the time, and God will bring good out of bad situations. However, recognize the enemy when he comes – don't confuse the enemy with God. It is not the will of God that you lose everything. Don't justify the bad things that happen. God is good all the time.

Jesus said, 'I have come that they might have life.' The Amplified version of the Bible uses the word 'enjoy' instead of 'have.' So take spiritual authority and enjoy your marriage, enjoy your family, enjoy your job, enjoy your ministry and enjoy full health. If you aren't enjoying life then read God's Word, mediate on it day and night and allow his nature to permeate your thinking. It's his will that we enjoy life. Let's show people who are not following Christ that we are people living life to the full and in overflowing abundance, not only when things are good but also when we face trials and tribulations.

Receive the Anointing

The proof of anointing is not trembling and falling over. Instead it's the releasing of burdens and the removal of yokes. Anointing will change you; it will strengthen you and underpin you. You will become free to keep moving forward, knowing that the past can be erased and that the chains of the enemy can be broken. Words that people have said to you in the past will dissolve into nothing. Burdens that you have carried for years can be lifted off you. Seek the anointing of God by standing in his presence in worship, praying, meditating on the Word and receiving the peace that he brings.

Prophetic Words

My dream of owning a chain of hotels resurfaced when a man I respect prophesied a word he believed was from God. It's a dangerous thing to live your life chasing after a dream based on something someone said; you risk looking a fool in front of people as you are putting your faith in something that was said rather than in the reality that surrounds you. It's even more dangerous when that word is spoken as a prophetic word, because now you have to decide if it is from God.

We are living in a season of renewed prophetic and spiritual gifting. In such a season there are many people who may speak words they genuinely believe are from God when, in actual fact, their words are merely from humans. A true prophetic word will align itself with the Word of God; it will reflect the very character, nature and person of Jesus Christ, which, in short, is love. The word will magnify and exalt God and, importantly, bring peace to the receiver and not confusion. So if you receive a prophetic word, don't feel compelled to take it at face value; meditate on it and ask yourself if you are at peace with it.

Prayerful Life

Earlier in the book I said that you don't have to pray constantly about your destiny. I need to clarify this point, because I don't want you to misinterpret what I am saying. I am certainly not encouraging you not to pray. Far from it – prayer is an essential part of your Christian life. Let your prayers acknowledge God, the creator of the heavens and the earth, the one who has blessed you with life, the Father who will move mountains because of faith. Ask for wisdom as you make key decisions, and thank him as you triumph over every hurdle. Ensure that every step you make is secure in the assurance that you have spoken to the heavenly Managing Director.

I recommend that you spend quality time every day in the presence of God. There are vital answers to your questions that you will receive in his presence. Prayer is a two-way communion, so, as much as you speak, be prepared to listen when you pray. If you are able to, pray in tongues, as the people did in Acts 2. Speaking in tongues is a gift from the Holy Spirit, which enables our inward spirit to commune directly with the Father. We must always pray with truth, the truth that is rooted in Scripture. Open up your Bible and pray through the Scriptures. Declare what the Word says in your prayers.

Honour God in Your Tithing and Giving

In times of economic recession, or when circumstances are difficult, it might seem rational to stop tithing and reduce your giving. But actually this is the time you need to maintain your giving – even increase it. It might seem strange, and most bank managers would probably think you are mad, but tithing and giving is often a good indication of your faith levels. Do you believe that God is your Jehovah-Jireh, your God of provision?

Before troubles even come, it is best to learn to operate in the principles of tithing and giving. As you pursue your dreams, you will be aware that God has promised protection and provision for those who trust him by giving their tithes and their offerings:

> 'Bring the whole tithe into the storehouse, that there may be food in my house. Test me in this,' says the LORD Almighty, 'and see if I will not throw open the floodgates of heaven and pour out so much blessing that you will not have room enough for it'.
>
> Mal. 3:10

There are plenty of Scriptures in the Old Testament that indicate that tithing was an obligation. With Jesus freeing us from legalism, we are now free to make our own choices. However, I personally think that tithing is a good discipline to follow, and any other offerings are gifts over and above that. I urge you to constantly allow the Spirit of God to impress on your heart to whom, when, and how much to give as an offering, whether it's financially, or through volunteering your time or in your relationships. As you give, you will see the blessings of God become evident in your life:

Give, and it will be given to you. A good measure, pressed
down, shaken together and running over, will be poured
into your lap. For with the measure you use, it will be meas-
ured to you.

Luke 6:38

In this chapter we have looked at building faith in your
life so that you can keep running and pursuing your
dream. Building faith means getting into the Word, thinking what is right, speaking what is right, and living in
obedience to the commands and promises God has given
us. The result of living by renewed faith will mean you
take spiritual authority over circumstances you
encounter, and you will receive anointing which will
remove the yokes and burdens that inhibit your life and
allow you to soar even higher, to reach your destiny.

10

Tools to Achieve Your Dreams
Part Two: Practical Steps

In the middle of difficulty lies opportunity.
Albert Einstein

I want to highlight some very practical things that you can do to help you achieve your dreams. It's down to you to take action; no one else will do it for you. You are responsible for what you become and what you achieve. You need to start taking practical steps to fulfil your dreams – form a plan and put in milestones that you can work towards. Where do you want to be in ten years' time? What job do you want to be doing? Where do you want to live? All these questions have answers and you can achieve them by planning, in the assurance that God will bless your steps as you allow him to lead you and guide you.

Write Down Your Dreams

In 1952, Yale University did a study of graduating business students. They were asked if they had written down any of their goals. Only three per cent of those who replied said they did. Twenty years later, the net worth of that three per cent was greater than the combined net worth of the other ninety-seven per cent of students. Since learning about this study, I have always written down my dreams. I started at the age of fifteen and I have never stopped. When we got married, my wife and I wrote down some joint dreams, most of which we have now achieved.

At the end of every year, I also complete a list of everything significant that I have achieved, including things that I had once dreamt about that I have since fulfilled. I then list some specific things that I want to see accomplished the following year. I have a spreadsheet of every list I have written since I was a teenager. It's a record of my achievements, a bank of examples of things that I have done that acts as an encouragement to me when thinking about what I want to do in the future; proof that I can do the things I set my mind to. Writing down your dreams will give them substance and will affect your future. Remembering what you have achieved will push you forward because you know God has been on your side.

Focus on Your End Game

After writing your dream down, concentrate on it in everything you do. You might have written down that you want to get married (this is just an example, there are some people who are called to be single). You may have a vision of what your future spouse looks like and what character traits they will posses, but marriage itself is the ultimate goal, the end game. Keep this in mind. In his various books Stephen Covey, a business writer, calls this keeping the main thing the main thing, or first things first. Or run 'with one focus' as Paul the apostle puts it:

> I do not consider, brethren, that I have captured and made it my own . . . but one thing I do [it is my one aspiration]: forgetting what lies behind and straining forward to what lies ahead, I press on toward the goal to win the supreme and heavenly prize to which God in Christ Jesus is calling us upward.
>
> Phil. 3:13,14, AMP

Paul finished the race. His goal was to preach Christ to the masses. He won the prize because he kept the main thing the main thing. Someone once said that greatness is the result of single-mindedness pursuing a primary objective. In 1970, Dr Edward Banfield of Harvard University conducted a study to discover what made certain people successful. He believed family background and education would prove to be the key factors, but he found that the most common characteristic among those who were successful was a long-term perspective. They had a clear dream. Keep your long-term perspective in front of you.

Count the Cost

Before you set off down the road in pursuit of your dream, you must count the cost. Not just how much it will cost you financially, but how much it will cost you emotionally and physically. You need to consider the strain on your family, friends and job. Do you have what it takes to finish the course? Don't be a person who starts a race and never finishes. If your heart is not in it, you will be handicapped before you start and will inevitably suffer disappointment. Be in it to win it, pursue your dreams with all that is within you. Don't set off thinking you can quit if things get hard.

A lot of people experience what is often called burn-out. Burn-out occurs when the pressure becomes too much, or something unexpected comes that totally destroys the dream. You can avoid burn-out and overcome any hurdle that gets in your way if you plan before you set out and are determined to see your dream fulfilled.

Set Intermediate Goals

It's great to have a big dream. But without an idea about the interim steps you need to take to reach it, you will, in all likelihood, fail. What are the key milestones between point 'A', where you are today, and point 'B', your dream? Can you break down the dream into smaller goals? Start with the end in mind and work back. If the dream is to own ten hotels, can you start by working in a bed and breakfast somewhere, or going into partnership with someone who wants to run one? You may not hit every goal you set, but that should not deter you. You need to keep going, revaluating and learning from your mistakes. Thomas Edison said, 'Many of life's failures are men who did not realize how close they were to success when they gave up.' If you don't keep going after you miss a goal you will never make it to the finishing line.

I run with a friend every week. We have been running the same four-mile course for the past three years. We started off running it in just over forty minutes (in our defence, it's through woodland and up very steep hills).

We now complete the same route in less than thirty minutes. To get to that level we have had to plan, to pace ourselves. First we split the course into three sections, which eventually got our time down to thirty-three minutes. Then we divided it into five sections, each of us taking it in turns to lead. In those smaller chunks, the course is more manageable and the little successes we achieve in completing each leg make the end result more satisfying.

Be Prepared

Now that you have set the goals and the intermediate milestones, you can start preparing yourself in advance. There's a military motto: 'proper prior preparation prevents poor performance' – you can never be over-prepared. We live in a competitive, fast-moving world. You need to prepare yourself ahead of time for the different tasks, jobs and projects that need to be accomplished at every milestone. If this requires going to night school or attending seminars, then this is what you need to do. If you are going after a new job, then read up on the company you are applying to. Whenever I attend interviews, I find out who is on the panel interviewing me, search for their name on the Internet and read up about them. Knowledge is key. The Scouts have got it right with their motto: 'Be prepared'.

Discipline Yourself: Form Habits

The only place where success comes before work is in the dictionary. In pursuit of your dreams, you may need to change your lifestyle, or learn something new, or even budget more. All these things require behaviour changes that take discipline to maintain. To achieve your dream, you are going to have to face up to challenges. Discipline is hard work. Thomas Edison said, 'Genius is one per cent inspiration, ninety-nine per cent perspiration.' Boxers know that champions are never made in the ring; they are just rewarded there, so their energies are put into the rigorous training and disciplined lifestyle. Every golfer wants to swing a club like Tiger Woods, but not everyone wants to get up at four a.m. to practise the same stroke over and over again. That kind of dedication takes discipline. Disciplining yourself will mean that you form positive habits that will become a part of your lifestyle and, in turn, help you to achieve your dream.

Keep Learning

One of my favourite quotes is from Gandhi, who said, 'Live as if you will die tomorrow, and learn as if you will live forever.' You can never know too much. You must consistently acquire understanding, wisdom and knowledge. Ignorance is every person's mountain. If you can become an expert in your chosen field, you will progress. Excellence comes from learning.

When I had a surf shop in Leeds, I had quite a few hours each day when the number of customers was low. Instead of sitting at the cash register watching surf movies, I decided to do a couple of London School of Theology modules. If you have time on your hands, the best thing you can do is learn, and if you can study the Word of God, then that's a winning combination. Gaining understanding will set you up for achieving your goals and ultimately your dream.

Get Around People You Admire

Our destiny is often tied up with other people. We live in a world that is bound by relationships. Genealogies in the Bible (those lengthy lists of an individual's antecedents) may seem laborious, but they remind us that we are never alone. Not only should we be proactive in the pursuit of our dreams, but we also need to be interactive with the people we admire and the people that cross our paths. If you are humble enough to appreciate that you can't do everything on your own, your challenges won't be so hard to overcome. Every problem that you face has probably been solved by someone else.

If you can find one or two people that you really admire, and they are able to give you time, then it will help you to enlarge your thinking. I have one person I regularly contact who owns a couple of hotels. This has proved extremely beneficial in the pursuit of my dream. I also have someone who I respect in my chosen profession. These people are further down the road than I am, so it helps to talk with them about the difficulties I am facing. It also allows me to question them on how they achieved their goals. Often they have overcome the same hurdles, so I learn from the mistakes they made and reach my goal quicker.

In terms of my faith, there have been various people I have seen as mentors, people who are examples of how to walk with God. You must find someone who can disciple you, and you must be prepared to disciple other people as well. One day you may need to pass the baton to someone else.

You may be surprised at who supports your dream. People you expect to back you up may distance themselves, because associating with someone who has a big dream brings with it potential consequences, especially if the dream is risky or out of the ordinary. But others who you did not expect to be an encouragement may turn out to be your best allies.

Evaluate Your Life

Balance in life is absolutely vital. Your time on earth is short, and it's easy to miss out on seeing your children grow up (if you have them), on your relationship with family and friends, or your relationship with God. Pursuing your dream should never be at the expense of any of these things, especially your relationship with God. But we shouldn't neglect the other aspects of life.

David Yonggi Cho, senior pastor and founder of the world's largest congregation, the Yoido Full Gospel Church in North Korea, was once asked why a particular move of God led by another minister had come to an abrupt end. He simply said, 'He should have played more golf.' You might have expected him to have talked about prayer or other aspects of spirituality, but he spoke about an earthly pastime and he was right. Even in ministry you need to have a work-life balance.

In an effort to ensure a balance in my life, I constantly evaluate the things I am involved in. I question why I devote myself to certain things, how much time they take out of my life and whether there is anything more important I could be doing. It is useful to ask yourself what TV shows and films you are watching, how much time you're spending with your family and friends, and how much in prayer and devotion. Pursuing your dream is great, but not at the expense of your family life and your relationship with God.

Be Careful in Your Decision-Making

Finally, I want to highlight something that was painful for me to learn. That is, how you make decisions in life. Every decision you make has a consequence, from the emails you write to which house you buy. Some of life's everyday decisions have the biggest consequences. You need to be careful that these decisions are not made in fear, defensively, or as a knee-jerk reaction. How do you ensure you don't make these types of decisions? Often it is simply a case of slowing down, of not reacting on the spur of the moment.

In the past, one of my biggest mistakes was always to answer emails immediately. I would often read an email without trying to understand the perspective of the person who wrote it. I had to learn to take time out before I responded. Since ninety-three per cent of communication is about how something is said, rather than what is said, written words are especially open to misinterpretation. It is better to slow down, to think about your decisions and, often, to talk them through with someone else before you set them in stone. Having done that, it is essential that you make a decision without procrastinating.

Taking these practical steps will put you in a strong position. Sometimes you can plan perfectly, take all the necessary steps and do everything by the book and life still gets in the way of your best intentions. You can do everything right but something still goes wrong. It's not necessarily your fault, it's just life. However, how you choose to deal with the setbacks that inevitably come your way – whether you take flight or stand up and fight – will determine your future.

11

Dealing with Failures: Fight or Flight?

> Far better it is to dare mighty things to win glorious triumphs, even though chequered with failure, than to take rank with those poor spirits who neither enjoy much nor suffer much, because they live in the grey twilight that knows not victory or defeat.
>
> Theodore Roosevelt

What happens when we have pursued a dream only to find we miss out? It's so easy for unfulfilled dreams to lead to despair or disillusionment. Imagine the violin soloist who has trained since the age of four. She has always dreamed of standing on stage in front of an orchestra but, even though she has studied hard, she still hasn't succeeded and now it seems her opportunity has passed. What will we say to her, what will motivate her now? Having a dream motivates us on a Monday morning but when that dream has been dashed, how do we get out of bed and keep going? I want to encourage everyone who has pursued their dreams only to find them disappear into despair that it doesn't have to mean the end. It is OK to fail! But the choices we make after we experience failure will dictate what happens next.

Failure is often a sign that you are going somewhere in life. In fact, there would be cause for concern if life wasn't chequered with problems and challenges. As you overcome each challenge, you will find your spirit is lifted and your faith rises. It's no wonder that James says that he rejoiced (Jas 1:2), not because of the trial, but for the greater glory that is given to God as he came out the other end. Can you say 'I will finish my course, I will fulfil my destiny'? Like Paul, can you say with conviction 'I run my life to gain the prize? (1 Cor. 9:24) As you go through difficulties and you continue to live in faith, you will find that God becomes more important than the dream – not that you will stop pursuing the dream.

Ralph Waldo Emerson, the American philosopher and poet, said that 'men succeed when they realize that their failures are the preparation for their victories'. Some of humankind's highest achievers, some of the most powerful men and women, in business, politics and sport, had to overcome dramatic failures to write their names in the history books. More than that, in many cases, they first had to fail before they could succeed. Thomas Edison produced over ten thousand unsuccessful prototypes before he finally demonstrated the first working light bulb on 21 October 1879. When a reporter asked, 'How did it feel to fail 10,000 times?' Edison replied, 'I didn't fail 10,000 times, the light bulb was an invention with 10,000 steps.' He had learned that from every failure comes the seed of an even greater potential success. As Albert Einstein said, 'Anyone who has never made a mistake has never tried anything new.' Your future is not determined by your past failures, but by your present decisions. We need to get over our failures, pick ourselves up and keep going.

During recent turbulent economic times, we have been shown the folly of putting all our confidence in the global financial institutions. Hardship is nothing new. Right at the beginning of the Bible, in Genesis 26, we read that there was famine in the land. Any farmer will tell you that some years bring a bumper harvest and others, a smaller one. Weather patterns change, economies go up and down; everything has a cycle. We really shouldn't be shocked by it. Failures happen, challenges and problems come and go. But one thing is constant – God will sustain us through it all:

> The steps of a [good man] are directed and established by the LORD when He delights in his way [and He busies Himself with his every step]. Though he falls, he shall not be utterly cast down, for the LORD grasps his hand in support and upholds him.
>
> Ps. 37:23,24, AMP

When I started writing this book, I didn't have many personal stories of failure. But the events of the last year have been the hardest of my life. I'd like to share them as an encouragement to you that it is possible to hit rock bottom and still believe in your dream and your destiny.

Going back to my school years, I was in all the bottom sets at high school and even had to go to special remedial English classes. 'Remedial': what a label to give someone at such an impressionable age. But I overcame my struggles at school and went on to college to study business. From there I went to university and, to many people's amazement, gained my bachelor's degree. After university I joined a chemical distribution firm, which I soon left to fulfil one of my earliest dreams – to start a surf shop. A year later, the landlords decided to refurbish the shops where I had my outlet and, as a result of the building work, trade dropped off and I decided to close up. I then joined a newspaper firm where I became their first buyer, purchasing goods and services for the business.

While I was with the paper, I started studying for the graduate diploma at the Chartered Institute of Purchasing and Supply, which led to me joining a major hotel chain as their buyer and, subsequently, to me becoming their senior buyer. I was then headhunted by a global company to lead their UK, Middle East and North Africa operations. My family and I moved to the south of England and I set up an operating company to facilitate the role. Up to this point, I had experienced the kinds of ups and downs that any budding entrepreneur goes through – no stratospheric highs, but no disastrous lows. There were difficult moments, like the decision to move south, away from our family and friends, but we approached these moments in faith and really felt God's hand on our lives from the beginning. In many ways it had been quite a smooth ride.

However, more recently we have faced the biggest battle of our lives. I became embroiled in a legal dispute that threatened to bankrupt us. In the year or so that followed we used all our savings to defend ourselves, and we had no income – we were therefore on the brink of total loss. But in that time we have learned things that might have taken a lifetime to grasp. We learned that we need people to speak the Word of God over us, to remind us that God is bigger than the disaster we faced. We didn't want sympathy or hollow claims that everything would be all right. We needed the solid Word that would instil in us hope and give us perseverance.

When you are on the verge of losing everything, you find out what really matters in life. We understood that it really didn't matter what was taken from us because our life isn't determined by material wealth. Life is more than just that.

We started to declare and decree that we would not lose everything. We reminded ourselves daily that God is the God of justice, that he will never let go of our hands, and that we had everything we needed to endure and to overcome the challenge.

Perhaps the hardest lesson I had to learn was about how to keep my dreams alive. In the face of losing everything, they had been ripped from under me. I faced failure in the world's eyes. However, failure doesn't have to be terminal; it doesn't have to mean the end of our dreams and, importantly, it doesn't mean we are being judged by God.

The apostle Paul failed many times over – he was shipwrecked and imprisoned. If a person's problems and failures mean they are living outside of the will of God for their life, then Paul was miles away from God's purpose for his. Problems, challenges and failures are all part of life's journey, and will hone your character and your faith. In the book of James, Paul assures us that no trial will overtake us that isn't known by God. God will offer you a way out. He has equipped you to overcome the trial:

> No temptation has seized you except what is common to man. And God is faithful; he will not let you be tempted beyond what you can bear. But when you are tempted, he will also provide a way out so that you can stand up under it. 1 Cor. 10:13

Failure may even present a great opportunity to revaluate what is important to us. Whatever we conclude, we need to remember that God's love for us is unconditional, and failure does not alter that. He wants us to learn from our failures as well as our successes, and be built up in faith, wisdom and understanding. His love for us is unchanging and everlasting (Jer. 31:3). God loves us the same yesterday, today, tomorrow and the day after that.

My legal battle ended in an out-of-court settlement. It meant that I didn't get the money I was owed, but it brought to a halt the process that could have resulted in me being made bankrupt.

The experience caused me to revaluate my hotel-chain dream. We no longer had the business that would have supported my ambition, and I had never felt further from achieving it. But I have also never stopped dreaming. I don't know how the future will take shape, but I know that it is rife with opportunity and I know that God has a plan. He knew my desires before I faced catastrophe, and he still knows them. And I know that he loves me. I will not quit. I am now in the process of negotiating a lease on a hotel. The dream isn't a reality yet, but I am taking steps to see it realised.

I hope this is an encouragement to you. Don't give up. Recognize that God is in the battle with you, you aren't in it on your own. You don't have to handle everything by yourself. With God you can endure the challenge and expect to receive something better. We are told in the Bible that Jesus endured the cross for joy (Heb. 12:2). He faced death head-on because he knew a new day would come. I can't urge you enough to get stuck into the Word, because it you will renew your strength. Meditate on God's Word:

But his delight is in the law of the LORD, and on his law he meditates day and night. He is like a tree planted by streams of water, which yields its fruit in season and whose leaf does not wither. Whatever he does prospers.

Ps. 1:2,3

Failure Is Not From God

A common misunderstanding people have of God is that he puts us through trials and tribulations in life to teach us a lesson. I want to tell you that failure is not from God. Cancer, debt, financial ruin – these are not God's will for our lives, although, sometimes God allows them to happen, unfortunately we don't know why.

As Christians, we are not immune from these things. However, God can help us in whatever trials we face and all things can be worked for good. Through his Word and his Spirit, we have everything we need to sustain us through the challenge. God is faithful.

By the same token, every challenge should not be viewed as the work of Satan. Trials are a fact of life: some children are as good as gold, others are hard work; some people face redundancy in every job they are in, some breeze through life in the same job. Everyone faces different challenges at different times in their life. We don't get to pick which ones we will have to deal with. Our trials are not unique to us – someone else has gone through exactly the same thing at some point. If they have made it, you can make it too.

Reflection

When you feel close to fulfilling your dream and something gets in the way that stops you from making progress, don't blame other people or try to dodge your failure. The best thing you can do is go to God. Like a perfect earthly father, he might congratulate you for coming as far as you have, but he may also show you areas for improvement and mistakes you need to learn from. And remember, he accepts you, whatever you have done.

Listen to what God is teaching you through each setback, because next time it happens you will know how to handle it. If someone else experiences the same thing, you will be able to help them through it. Any conquered challenge will give you a fresh opportunity to start over in greater wisdom.

As well as reflecting and listening to God, you will benefit from talking through your failures with a trusted friend or church leader. Failure in itself isn't sin, however, sin, such as disobedience, may have been the root cause. Failure often affects others around you, so be honest and always be willing to say sorry. Learning from failure by talking it through with people of maturity and wisdom can provide you with your own spiritual momentum and maturity.

Anchor yourself in God's hope and whatever trial or tribulation you are facing will pass. When it looked as if I was losing everything, I reminded myself that I would still see my children's birthdays and that Christmas was still on my calendar. I reminded myself that God was still on my side every time I saw the sunrise.

12

Go!

The pessimist complains about the wind, the optimist
expects it to change; the realist adjusts the sails.
William Arthur Ward

I want to finish simply by encouraging you and praying for
you – that God fills your heart with dreams, and that your
faith will give you the courage and the strength to pursue
them. So go and find your dream, and then chase it with all
your might. God has placed hidden treasures in you – now
it's up to you to do something. We all know that life is hard
and, consequently, it's easy for us to ignore our dreams and
simply drift, hoping that things will be different, without
actively doing anything to effect change. But you have the
ability, the power and, if you surrender to Jesus, the support
you need to take control of your life. Will you be a drifter,
or will you make the decision to adjust your sails so that
you can step into the dreams that God has given you?

Everyone faces difficulties and crises. You should never
assume your life is the hardest, or your situation unique.
There is always someone else who has gone through the
same trials and tribulations, and they have triumphed. So
let that be an inspiration. You can succeed; you can overcome your trials.

Some dreams are never achieved. However, that should not stop you conceiving new dreams. It's easy to allow the disappointments and hurt of lost dreams to overshadow new dreams, but it's your decision to either take flight or keep fighting. God has not changed; he is still on the throne. It's time for you to rise again, get that glint back in your eye and know that, with every sunrise, God is still on your side. God really does care about your dreams and he wants to bless you. All he asks of you is that your honour him, please him in your actions and that you love him wholeheartedly. If you didn't make it at first, keep trying.

In pursuit of your dreams, you may discover that your character needs work. God changes us by his Spirit to be more like him, but we need to allow ourselves to be changed. This is solely down to us; we are responsible for responding to the Spirit and developing our character. We can't blame God for something not happening in our lives if it's our character that's stopping us:

> If you grow a healthy tree, you'll pick healthy fruit. If you grow a diseased tree, you'll pick worm-eaten fruit. The fruit tells you about the tree.
>
> Matt. 12:33, MSG

This paraphrased Scripture starts with the words 'If you', showing that we are ultimately responsible for growing the healthy tree. God gives us the tools and Spirit that will help and guide us, but we need to allow the Spirit to change our character so we bear healthy fruit.

The way to change your character is by meditating on the Word and allowing the Spirit to change your mindset and attitude. You will only reach the altitude of your attitude. The eagle and the turkey are fundamentally the same: they both have wings, they both have beaks, but one rules the skies and the other is destined for the oven. Do you want to soar with eagles or hang around turkeys eating barnyard feed? If you want to soar like an eagle, get around people who inspire you and consistently speak the Word of God to you; even change the church you are attending if you need to. Ask yourself, 'What am I feeding myself with?' Stay in the Word, in good times and in bad. Don't just go to church when the trials come. Grounding yourself in faith, amongst God's people, in good times, will give you the solid foundations to endure the bad times. Faith motivated by fear is flawed.

At the end of this chapter I have included a set of questions that will help you plan your next steps to achieving your dreams. Use them to complete a plan for pursuing your dream. Consider your life's dreams and write down the key milestones that you can aim for, the hurdles and challenges you might face and how you can overcome them. You could also draw or cut pictures out from magazines as a collage of your dream map.

What can you do now? Enrol in night school? Get into better physical shape? You may need to clear your overdraft and get on top of your finances. You may need to rebuild a bridge with someone from your past. Whatever steps you need to take, God will direct your paths and make your way straight. Pour the water on the hidden painting and the picture will be revealed.

Keep going. Like a boxer, you need to snap out your jab and fight. Don't quit, don't shrink back, keep persevering and you will gain faith, hope and confidence:

So do not throw away your confidence; it will be richly rewarded. You need to persevere so that when you have done the will of God, you will receive what he has promised.

For in just a very little while, 'He who is coming will come and will not delay. But my righteous one will live by faith. And if he shrinks back, I will not be pleased with him.' But we are not of those who shrink back and are destroyed, but of those who believe and are saved.

Heb. 10:35–39

You will always face obstacles and challenges in your life. The only people doing things perfectly are those who are doing nothing at all. Don't give up, don't throw away your confidence; endure the race set before you. Faith won't get you into a difficult situation, but it will get you out. As you overcome each hurdle, keep the level of new-found faith in the same place because in the aftermath of a victory your guard will come down. Like a boxer who wins a fight, after the victory comes tiredness.

When the challenges you face feel like rejection, think of them as an opportunity to head in a new direction. As one door shuts, another will open. Life might feel full of Garden of Eden snakes and Jacob's ladders: dreams that move us closer to our destiny and temptations that may offer the promise of good things in the moment, but that result in us going backwards. Recognize the snakes and focus on the ladders, so that you can continue to move forward in your dream.

In the first chapter I quoted John Barrymore: 'A man is not old until regrets take the place of dreams.' This quote was what really encouraged me when I first started to consider this book. I will never stop dreaming and pursuing my dreams because it will mean I will have grown tired and old. Stop dreaming and you stop truly living.

I will always remember something I was told when I was younger: 'There is a hidden treasure in you and it needs to come out.'

There is a treasure in you, too. Go and fulfil your dreams.

My Dream Plan

What are my long-term dreams?

What are the specifics of my dream?

What are the key milestones on the way to achieving my dream?

What challenges do I foresee that may stand in the way of my dream? (Finances, qualifications, etc.)

Do I need to learn anything new? What can I do now to prepare myself?

What character traits do I need to work on?

Which people do I admire that I can call on to support me?

Which people can I disciple?

How can I support my spouse's dreams (if married)?

Dream Collage

There is an example of a dream collage on the previous page. Use the space below to draw pictures or cut out images from magazines as a collage of your dream map.

Notes

[1] 'Episode 21: Chuck Versus the Colonel' in *Chuck*, Season 2 (College Hill Pictures, 2009).

[2] Author unknown.

[3] Dr C.A. Dollar, *8 Steps to Create the Life You Want: The Anatomy of a Successful Life* (New York: FaithWords, 2008), p. 251.

[4] *Cool Runnings* (Walt Disney, 1993).

Bibliography

Bannatyne, D., *Anyone Can Do It: The Autobiography* (London: Orion, 2006).

Covey, S.R., *The 7 Habits of Highly Effective People: Restoring the Character Ethic* (London: Simon & Schuster, 1999).

'Episode 21: Chuck Versus the Colonel' in *Chuck*, Season 2 (College Hill Pictures, 2009).

Damazio, F., *10 Secrets of a Successful Achiever* (Portland, OR: CityBible Publishing, 2003).

Dollar, Dr C.A., *8 Steps to Create the Life You Want: The Anatomy of a Successful Life* (New York: FaithWords, 2008).

Gladwell, M., *Outliers: The Story of Success* (London: Penguin Books, 2009).

Joyner, R., *Fifty Days for a Soaring Vision: a Fifty-Day Devotional for a Foundation Built on Solid Biblical Principles* (Charlotte, NC: MorningStar Publications, 2001).

Liardon R., *Smith Wigglesworth: The Complete Collection of His Life Teachings* (New Kensington, PA: Whitaker House, 2008).

Matthew, D., *Dead Dreams Can Live* (Bradford: Harvestime, 1987).

'Episode 13: The Fix' in *Heroes*, Season 1 (NBC Universal Television, 2009).

Rosenthal, M., *The Character Factory: Baden-Powell and the Origins of the Boy Scout Movement* (London: Collins, 1986).

Swift, A.J., *My Reason For Hope* (Milton Keynes: Authentic Media, 2008).

Cinderella (Walt Disney, 1950).

Cool Runnings (Walt Disney, 1993).

Warner, W., ed., *The Anointing of His Spirit: Smith Wigglesworth* (Ann Arbor, Mich: Vine Books,1994).

Washington, J.M., ed., *I Have a Dream: Writings and Speeches That Changed the World* (San Francisco: Harper SanFrancisco, 1992).